CLASSIC TT RACERS

GREG PULLEN

CLASSIC TT RACERS

THE GRAND PRIX YEARS 1949–1976

THE CROWOOD PRESS

First published in 2019 by
The Crowood Press Ltd
Ramsbury, Marlborough
Wiltshire SN8 2HR

www.crowood.com

British Library Cataloguing-in-Publication Data
A catalogue record for this book is available from the British Library.

ISBN 978 1 78500 629 6

Designed and typeset by Guy Croton Publishing Services,
West Malling, Kent

Printed and bound in India by Parksons Graphics

CONTENTS

INTRODUCTION

If you love motorcycles then the Isle of Man will be somewhere you've either visited, or plan to go to one day. Consider the long-lost factories of Norton, Velocette, Rudge, BSA, Triumph, AJS and all the rest: the TT is where these British firms built their world domination, and the TT is where Honda went first to steal it away from them.

Indian raced at the TT to prove they could build better motorcycles than Harley-Davidson, and Moto Guzzi taught the world that rear suspension was a good idea on the Isle of Man. The mountain course is where Norton debuted Borrani alloy rims – painted black to fool the competition into thinking they were plain old steel – and where the Gilera and MV Agusta fours were first taken when it was time to test them in competition outside their native Italy. Velocette developed the positive stop foot-change gearbox and Rudge the radial 4-valve head primarily to win at the TT.

For sixty or seventy years the Isle of Man TT races were simply the most important motorcycle races in the world. When a motorcycle road racing championship was proposed in 1948 there was never any doubt that the Isle of Man TT would be a part of it. From the start of the motorcycle World Championships in 1949 the TT classes became must-win races for both riders and factories. Whatever it took to win – money, a better rider, a new technology – it was taken to the Isle of Man. Eventually the mountain course would prove too challenging – read 'dangerous' – to remain part of the World Championship and 1976 was the last year in which TT results counted towards the various titles. This is the story of some of the motorcycles that raced in those twenty-eight years, and of a very special mountain course.

Inevitably any research project is as good as those who support it. I am especially indebted to Pat Slinn, who first visited a TT in 1948 – his father was there to develop a new BSA swing arm in the Clubman's Junior TT. Pat returned as a BSA apprentice in 1958 and has visited the Island's races every year since. He has worked with Ducati over the course of five World Championships for Mike Hailwood and Tony Rutter. Pat's introductions to TT legends – he grew up calling Geoff Duke 'Uncle Geoff' – have been invaluable. So, too has his friend Bill Snelling who never returned from his first TT: he was so smitten with the racing and the island that he still lives there, the curator of a fabulous photographic archive that can be seen and bought via TTracepics.com.

Thanks must also go to the motorcycle team at Bonham's. I consult for them, but it is really for my knowledge of Italian motorcycles. Being able to ask Bonham's specialists about the Velocettes especially was very much appreciated, as are the photographs they have kindly allowed to be included. Finally, and most importantly, thanks to my wife Joanna. A writer's income is modest in the extreme and the hourly rate best not thought about. Yet Joanna makes sure I have the time and travel needed to complete works such as this, as well as encouragement. Without her and the wonderful stories that are there to be discovered this book would not have been finished. But I have enjoyed it, and hope every reader does as well.

This pretty valley is between two of the fastest parts of the TT course: Sulby Straight and Bungalow. Mike Hailwood once joked that his secret to a fast lap was to use the road through this valley as a short cut.

CHAPTER ONE

CREATING A LEGEND

While the rest of the world seemed happy to accept motorcycle and automobile racing on open roads, Britain was pretty much unique in absolutely prohibiting it. The 1903 Motor Car Act subjected the British to a blanket 20mph (32km/h) speed limit, despite warnings that the embryonic British motor industry was being stifled at birth. Reliability and performance could not be developed while it remained illegal to go faster than 20mph.

The ban became especially humiliating for British motoring enthusiasts when they realized that Selwyn Edge, who won the 1902 Gordon Bennett Cup, would be unable to defend his trophy on home soil as was traditional, and perhaps not at all. But the British Government held firm on the racing ban and speed limit and, with no purpose-built race tracks in existence, options were in short supply.

It's a near-death thing. Few realize that behind the scoreboard is a cemetery, with Snaefell in the distance.

Almost since the beginning the Island's Boy Scouts have acted as runners for the scoreboard.

Eventually a compromise was reached with the organizers and competing clubs, who agreed that the 'British' Gordon Bennett Cup of 1903 could be held in Athy, a market town in County Kildare in Ireland, some 50 miles (80km) south-west of Dublin. In gratitude to the Irish, the British team painted its car in a shamrock green livery and thus was created 'British' racing green.

But British motor sport couldn't stake its entire future on the generosity of the Irish. So Julian Orde, secretary of the Automobile Car Club of Britain and Ireland, persuaded the Tynwald (the Isle of Man's proudly independent government) to authorize the island's first motor race. The Isle of Man is not part of the United Kingdom, although it does enjoy the protection of the British government and, of course, geographically is part of the British Isles. So the High Court of Tynwald – believed to be the oldest continuous parliamentary body in the world – passed the 1904 Manx Highways (Light

Locomotive) Act, permitting a 52-mile (84km) 'Highlands' Course' to be used for the 1904 Gordon Bennett Eliminating Trial. This was won by Clifford Earl in a Napier, as was the 1905 trial that was held the following May.

THE FIRST TT

Gordon Bennett became wealthy through journalism and newspaper publishing in New York, although he was of Scottish heritage. Nothing was too outrageous or dangerous for him, his stunts and fabulous motor cars leading to people shouting 'Gordon Bennett!' after him, the origin of today's expression. Unsurprisingly he was soon using his connections and cash to start a fledgling motor car racing fraternity in Europe.

In September 1905 the Royal Automobile Club gladly jumped on Gordon Bennett's bandwagon with an event dubbed the

With your back to Snaefell there are the pits, a short walk to Douglas Promenade and the Irish Sea.

Isle of Man Tourist Trophy – soon abbreviated to the RAC TT. The island had its first TT, although not for motorcycles. Yet.

Having competed in the previous year's Gordon Bennett Cup, motorcycles were allowed to enter a sister event to the 1905 Gordon Bennett Eliminating Trial. The Manx government was persuaded to allow a motorcycle competition to take place the day after the automobile trial, to qualify riders for the International Motorcycle Cup that was due to be held in Austria in 1906.

The poor hill-climbing abilities of pioneering motorcycles led to the organizers switching the two-wheeled trial from the steep mountain roads of the Highlands Course to a less daunting 25-mile (40km) route. This ran south from Douglas to Castletown and then turned north to Ballacraine, before returning to a start/finish line at Quarterbridge in Douglas. The route included Crosby and Glen Vine, following part of today's current mountain course, albeit in the opposite direction. This 1905 event was that year's International Motorcycle Cup, and the five-lap, 125-mile (201km) race was won by J.S. Campbell on an Ariel. He therefore became part of the British

team to travel to the following year's International Motorcycle Cup in Austria.

Unhappily – or perhaps not, given what was to follow – the British riders who arrived in Austria were appalled at what they were found themselves asked to race against, and their collective disappointment would lead to the creation of the Isle of Man motorcycle TT.

Even before it started, the 1906 International Motorcycle Cup was plagued by recriminations. The wicked continentals were, the British claimed, cheating by bolting monstrous engines into flimsy chassis to create pure racing motorcycles that, while within the regulation weight restrictions, bore little resemblance to any production models available to the public.

This made the continentals' machines uncatchable in a straight line but, the British argued, would send motorcycle development down an – admittedly fast – blind alley. The host nation's Puch factory was openly using a mechanic riding a sidecar outfit stuffed with spares to shadow its riders. Even the French protested about that, but all complaints fell on deaf ears and were ignored by the sport's ruling body, the

Lap times are still-hand painted on the scoreboard.

Fédération Internationale des Clubs (FIC). This played a significant part in that organization being replaced by the Fédération Internationale de Motocyclisme (FIM), motorcycle racing's primary and overarching governing body to this day.

While today's racing fans might complain that manufacturers wield too much power over race organizers, it was ever thus as the demise of the FIC illustrates. Even in those early days the needs of manufacturers held sway in the real – but then rarefied – world of selling motorcycles. Pioneer manufacturers needed to prove to potential customers that their motorcycles offered robustness, good fuel economy and a modicum of comfort. Flimsy bicycles with heavyweight V-twin engines might win sprint races but they were, to British minds at the time at least, unlikely to promote and popularize motorcycling as an activity rather than as a spectator sport. After all, the industry was likely to sell far more motorcycles if everybody could join in.

So, on the long train journey home from Austria, Freddie Straight, the ambitious secretary of the British motorcycle sport's governing body, the ACC (Auto Cycle Club), the brothers Henry and Charlie Collier (owners of Matchless motorcycles) and the enthusiastic UK-based aristocrat, the Marquis de Mouzilly St Mars, discussed setting up an alternative to the International Motorcycle Cup.

They ultimately decided upon a race for road-legal motorcycles, based on the RAC TT, to be held on the Isle of Man. The final format was proposed by the editor of *The Motor Cycle* at the ACC's annual dinner in London on 17 January 1907. Competitors in the two classes would need to focus on fuel consumption – singles needing to average 90mpg (2.61ltr/100km) and twins 75mpg (3.14ltr/100km) – if they were to complete the course. Fuel would be measured into each entrant's tank at the start of the race to ensure compliance and, emphasizing the desire to develop touring motorcycles, there were regulations requiring the inclusion of saddles, tools, mudguards and silencers. In practice, riders would also choose to drape spare tyres and inner tubes across their shoulders in anticipation of the inevitable punctures.

The lowland circuit used for the International Cup on the Isle of Man in 1905 had proved gruelling and difficult to man-

The pits used to be on the other side of the slip road, right on the course; the current arrangement is far safer.

age, so the Auto Cycle Club, hubristically believing the British team would win in Austria, had already plotted out an alternative course for the following year's event. This, the St John's Course, was to be adopted for the first TT. The proposed route passed by the old open-air Manx Parliament site in St John's parish and the race started by the nearby school of that name. – this was fortuitous in that blackboards could be brought outside to record lap times. Across the road was an open field that was literally a paddock – for horses – that was set aside for marshalling and repairs. The name stuck, although these days horsepower rather than real horses is what motor sport fans expect to see in a race meeting's paddock.

Riding an anti-clockwise course, riders would head north towards Ramsey from Ballacraine to Kirk Michael, following some six miles of the current mountain course. Then they would double back along the coast to Peel, before returning to St John's. Altogether it was a 15.8-mile (25.4km) route designed to showcase rider and machine capability, rather than bring about a demolition derby.

The St John's course had roads that were narrower than those of the mountain course, especially the coast road that runs with the Irish Sea on the rider's right for many miles. Although lacking Snaefell's climbs, the St John's course challenged with sharper corners and ran through very few built-up areas. A ten-lap race was envisaged, with a compulsory ten-minute break at half distance. After all, these were the days when a rider was expected to be able to change a broken exhaust valve or ruined tyre and still go on to win a race.

With Britain failing to win the 1906 International Cup, by serendipitous good fortune plans were fully in place to host what the British felt would be an altogether better race. The inaugural international Isle of Man motorcycle races, which had been expected to be the 1907 International Cup, were ready to run as the first motorcycle TT even before it was called that.

And so on 28 May 1907 the TT was born to a cold, grey morning on the Isle of Man. At 10 o'clock the first riders pushed off on their 500cc single-cylinder Triumphs, Frank Hulbert and Jack Marshall riding away to Ballacraine, presumably oblivious of the historical significance of their actions. Ten laps and 158 miles later, Charlie Collier aboard a single-cylinder Matchless would be declared the victor. Averaging 38.2mph, he actually bested the performance of the winner of the 2-cylinder class, Rem Fowler, on a Peugeot-engined Norton. The Isle of Man was on its way to being one of the most famous destinations for motorcycle enthusiasts on earth, something that is perhaps more true today than it was in those pioneering days.

THE MOST BEAUTIFUL RACE COURSE ON EARTH?

Yet the first thing that must surely strike visitors to the Isle of Man, especially during the forty-eight weeks of the year when motorcycling largely abandons the island, is the breathtaking scenery. Sweeping, sandy beaches are sheltered by sheer rock faces that fall away inland, yielding up wooded springs and friendly paddling streams. Narrow lanes squeeze between fuchsia hedges and ancient stone walls as if they were tendrils of some long dead mycelium. Feral chickens ambush picnickers, making the most of the absence of foxes on this rock between Ireland and Great Britain. Then there is the mountain, Snaefell (Norse for 'snow mountain'), which can be brooding in swathes

of mist or majestically beautiful, particularly in late summer and autumn as the heather drapes the towering landscape in a purple cape. All the while the sheep stare benignly at visitors to one of the most beautiful and eerily peaceful places on earth.

Go there other than during the Southern 100, TT, Classic TT and Manx Grand Prix, and you might never realize the island has a great motorcycling heritage. Mona's Isle might be home to one of the most important, oldest and historic motorcycle racing courses on earth yet, in 2007 when its residents were invited to take part in celebrations marking the centenary of the first-ever motorcycle TT, many of the indigenous population didn't fully realize its international significance.

As with the Spa Francorchamps circuit in Belgium, no amount of time spent viewing on-board racing footage prepares you for experiencing the climbs and descents of the Isle of Man's mountain course at first hand. Even more shocking is that when a rider warns that a corner is blind, they don't just mean a late apex – they mean you ride with an open throttle alongside solid stonework, trusting absolutely that your recollection of what comes next isn't fatally flawed. Then, as you climb up into the clouds, it can feel as if you're about to launch skyward before you snap left – and there's the road again, cut into the green and black of Snaefell.

This is a Monza-esque, full-throttle red line of tarmac across

Winner of the twin-cylinder class of the first TT, Rem Fowler. IOMTT.COM

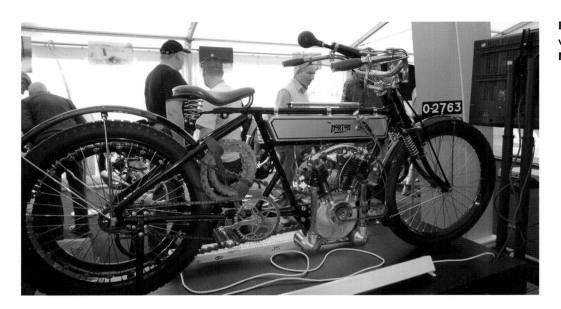

Rem Fowler's motorcycle was a Peugeot-engined Norton.

a mountainside that offers nothing but a steep and unforgiving drop punctuated by dry stone walling and rocky cuttings. But, unlike Monza, the TT course wasn't built for racing, but rather is a circular route of public roads co-opted to prove the worth of motorcycles and their riders. This is what makes it a course, rather than a circuit: the latter is a fixed and permanent racing venue, which means that you can ride a circuit of the course or just use it as part of the public highway. The pedantry of the English language!

The highest point of the course, near Brandywell, is some 422m (1,385ft) above sea level, lying in the shadow of Snaefell's 621m (2,037ft) summit which, in the clearest weather, allows you to plainly see five kingdoms: England, Ireland, Scotland, Wales and Heaven. It adds a dramatic dimension to the Island's emerald splendour.

But eventually you are brought back to earth, remembering Conor Cummins' crash up here in 2010. The top men aim 200bhp and nearly 200mph of rider and motorcycle between the faulted and folded sedimentary rocks, between houses and telegraph poles. Danger and exhilaration or, as Bianchi and Alfa Romeo racing legend Tazio Nuvolari put it, 'women and engines; joy and pain'.

Why do they do it? Because they love the challenge of the last traditional motor sport event on earth. Yet, although safety has improved beyond all recognition, the 4-cylinder bikes that largely rule the TT are now so quick that it seems the Senior TT is unlikely to ever run in rain again. So the TT remains undoubtedly the most dangerous sporting arena in the world, although Sammy Miller puts it more bluntly. The Irish-

man was a road racer of note at the TT, riding for Mondial and Ducati in the 1950s, before becoming famous as a trials maestro. This is what he has to say about the TT in the twenty-first century: 'Madness. 200mph through there? You've got no chance.' Yet reminded there were more fatalities in the sport when he was active in road racing, his thoughts on his fellow competitors are even more sobering. 'We could be losing one a week. Sometimes I don't think you need to think too much as a racer. You don't want to be flying along thinking "What if the gearbox gave up now?"'

It's odd to think how little human life was valued in the early years of the twentieth century. In the USA, board-track racing spectators would pay to be photographed next to dead riders and their machines, left where they fell to boost income for race organizers. Helmets were only thought of after T.E. Lawrence (Lawrence of Arabia) was killed on his Brough Superior, causing a young Hugh Cairns, one of Britain's first neurosurgeons, to start research on the head trauma suffered by motorcyclists when they crashed. A single-cylinder motorcycle with a handful of horsepower might seem unimpressive today, but was quite capable of killing a pioneering motorcycle racer. Even by the late 1960s the mountain course was unquestionably the most dangerous race track on earth. Horrendously tricky to learn, and brutally unforgiving of even minor errors, it is easy to understand why even the most fanatical motorcycle enthusiast might consider the TT a distasteful and unwelcome reminder of a bygone age: a time when human life was seen as a tradable and disposable commodity.

A rider might achieve greatness on the Isle of Man, but

Guthrie's Memorial on Snaefell, the mountain section of the course.

he stood a higher chance of being killed there than at any other sporting event in the world, a fact that remains unequivocally true today. The very nature of racing on closed roads racks up the odds of something going catastrophically wrong: machinery fails; conditions are unpredictable; stone walls are immovable. Inevitably, people die. Racing along public roads, flashing between buildings, speeding up and over a mountain before charging down to a rocky coast has never been less than hazardous, and motorcycle racers think only of glory and self-satisfaction in achievement, never believing it will be them who one day – perhaps even today – has to pay the ultimate price.

FREEDOM OF CHOICE – BUT SOMETIMES NOT

A rider chooses to submit himself (and occasionally herself) to the challenges of racing on the Isle of Man. But for a brief period many were given no choice. When the world motorcycling championships were first run in 1949, only two of the six rounds were held on purpose-built circuits, as opposed to courses that included closed public roads. These circuits were Monza in Italy and Bremgarten in Switzerland, but the latter banned most motor sport altogether after the 1955 disaster at Le Mans, when a car crashed into the crowds killing over eighty people.

But gradually the co-opted courses shrank to became

permanent circuits and much safer, while the Isle of Man remained, well, the Isle of Man. Yet as a round of the World Championship riders – especially if employed by a team or factory – were often obliged to race there. Inevitably, eventually one star too many was killed, Morbidelli's Italian rider Gilberto Parlotti, and the top riders sensed a change of mood. Parlotti had been a good friend of MV Agusta's superstar rider Giacomo Agostini, who led the revolt. His masters, also Italian, took his wishes to heart and, given that at the time riders could drop their poorest results from the season's final tally, it was less likely to affect World Championship standings than it would now.

Initially the sport's governing bodies, the international FIM and its British equivalent, the Autocycle Union (ACU), felt the stars would drift back or that factories would force riders' hands. It didn't happen and when the sports' newest and greatest superstar, Barry Sheene, made it plain that he would never return to the TT, the powers that be realized they were on the losing side. 1976 was the final year that the Isle of Man hosted a World Championship Grand Prix, Silverstone on the mainland being awarded the prize of hosting the British Grand Prix. Most thought that would bring an end to the TT races, but the return of Mike Hailwood in 1978 and 1979 reinvented the event. Ironically it now thrives, and has made stars of its greatest riders. Guy Martin is probably as well known as Valentino Rossi, and John McGuinness's and Michael Dunlop's names trip off motorcycle enthusiasts' tongues as readily as do those of most MotoGP stars.

Why does the TT still thrive? I would suggest that what

Museum and guardian up by Bungalow.

Almost at the highest point of the course riders enjoy the privilege of riding in the tyre tracks of heroes.

The Joey Dunlop memorial up above the Bungalow section of the course.

the TT and Classic TT offer is access. At a MotoGP event the spectator experience has been diluted beyond recognition, ostensibly in the name of safety but, older fans suspect, in the pursuit of profit and especially television coverage. When my generation started going to races in the mid 1970s there was a good chance of bumping into Barry Sheene, Kenny Roberts, Phil Read and Giacomo Agostini. That is unthinkable now, yet at the TT not only is there a fair chance of bumping into John McGuiness, there is also a fair chance he and wife Becky will stop and chat to you. And then when he's racing you can pick a viewing spot a few feet from the course and feel the rush of air as he passes.

You can also have little idea of what it is like to ride a MotoGP circuit on a MotoGP bike unless you have very deep pockets. But the TT course is always there, and on Mad Sunday the mountain section is one way only and speed limit free. Since the racers use motorcycles based on those in showrooms – albeit sometimes expensively modified but still closely related to what you can buy – you can get to know how deep a TT racer's talent goes, and briefly understand why they do it.

But why does the Isle of Man government do it? The TT is horrifically expensive to run: prize money alone is around £250,000, never mind the appearance fees and cost of ac-

tually running a race that involves preparing public roads for 200mph motorcycles. The answer is in the Great British holiday: like the equivalent United Kingdom coastal resorts the Isle of Man used to benefit hugely from tourism, a business now largely lost to Jumbo Jets and the sunny climes of southern Europe. But the Isle of Man has the TT races and today well over 40,000 people come to see them, some for a full fortnight. They pay for hotels, bed and breakfast, meals out and much more: the Isle of Man's autonomous status means that its government keeps all of the tax revenue so generated, which explains the TT's survival.

The chapters that follow are a history and tribute to some of the most important and successful motorcycles that raced during the TT's years as host of the British round of the motorcycle World Championship. The selection criteria were that the motorcycle must have at least secured a podium finish in the Senior (500cc) TT, then the Blue Riband class of the World Championship. A motorcycle that won a Senior TT during that era gets included automatically. Dominance in the only other race always run at the TT – the 350cc Junior – is also a reason for inclusion. Happily this gives a more-or-less chronological order that illustrates early dominance by British singles, the success of the Italian multis and the eventual rise of the 2-strokes and Japanese factories.

CHAPTER TWO

BRITISH SINGLE DOMINATION

It is hard to believe that shortly before its collapse in the 1970s BSA was building more motorcycles than any other factory in the world. Today all that is left of BSA's Birmingham factory is car repair workshops and such, plus a small building that has a BSA sign outside and still makes small arms, the origins of the name BSA (Birmingham Small Arms). There is nothing else to mark out one of the glories and stupidities that were shared between the British (in truth English) motorcycle industries.

BSA took its world dominance for granted, and the people who made the money had no interest in motorcycles or even in engineering. After a sales manager took lunch in the BSA's directors' dining room he was taken to one side and told he should never again bring riding attire into such hallowed quarters. BSA chairman Sir Bernard Docker allowed his wife

to order a Daimler (then – how the mighty fell – a subsidiary of BSA) with gold plating, ivory fittings and zebra-skin upholstery. This sort of behaviour was often funded by tax write-offs or simply designated as necessary company expenditure, ultimately costing Sir Bernard his position. It seems unlikely, however, that he and his fellow leaders of industry suffered from the collapse of the British motorcycle industry as much as those who actually built the motorcycles, owned dealerships or otherwise relied on Britain's world-beating factories. And of course everybody suffered when government found its tax revenues in freefall.

How this hubris came to pass is not difficult to see. France and Belgium had led the way in the early days of automotive design and manufacture, but the two world wars destroyed their early lead. Italy and Germany then took up the baton,

Despite building grand prix twins, Triumph achieved little at the TT during its years as the British Grand Prix.

BSA built arguably the most famous British single, but the Gold Star's origins as an off-road competition bike left it uncompetitive at the TT.

but again war left them in ruins. The British had an open goal and even dismissed lightweights from Japan and Italy as mere fodder for those just starting out, expecting riders to eventually graduate to a large-capacity British motorcycle. How wrong they were.

But while the post-war sun shone the British made hay. They had access to the huge demand from the USA, and riders who knew the TT course. This was – and this phrase will get repeated – the most important race in the world and, while riders came from all over the world, only those from the British Isles were able to compete year-in, year-out and so perfect their knowledge of the course. These masters of the mountain course were cherry-picked by the factories, and vice-versa: the best riders had the best machines. That legendary names such as Triumph and BSA are not included in the following chapters shows how hard those who could make a podium finish or even win were trying. BSA also learned a valuable lesson from the TT: to finish first, first you must finish. The TT started as a race intended to prove reliability at least as much as

speed. When BSA first took a factory team there in the 1920s not one of their motorcycles finished a race. Thereafter BSA focussed on off-road sport, most especially the magnificent World Championship achievements of Jeff Smith.

Triumph simply seemed to lack the machinery, pushrod ohv twins no match for the ohc singles of Velocette, Norton and AMC. Triumph did well at the Manx, winning the first post-war Senior race, but the Manx was a largely amateur event for sporting rather than racing motorcycles. Ironically it was after the TT lost its World Championship status that Triumph and BSA, working together on the 750cc 3-cylinder Trident and Rocket respectively, had their greatest successes. But by then the TT was in what looked like terminal decline. It was a far cry from the days when advertising was limited to a simple message, and there could be no greater strapline than a boast of TT wins. With the 1949 Senior TT was the opening round of the new motorcycle World Championship, there has perhaps never been a race that factories were more eager to win. This is the story of the greatest motorcycles of that age.

CHAPTER THREE

VELOCETTE KTT

Considering that Velocette was a family-owned business throughout its existence, and that the numbers of motorcycles it built were tiny in comparison with Norton and AJS, it is astounding that it was the only British factory besides those two marques to win a road-racing World Championship.

Velocette was largely created by a single German immigrant and his sons. In 1876, at the age of 19, Johannes Gutgemann came to England. He married Elizabeth Ore and they had two sons, Percy and Eugene, settling in Birmingham. Johannes initially adopted the English name John Taylor and, with William Gue, established Taylor-Gue Limited in 1905, selling cycle parts. A year later they were offering a complete motorcycle, the Veloce, after which Taylor struck out on his own, taking the Veloce name with him.

His two sons pursued engineering careers and founded New Veloce Motors in 1907, intending to build cars, but found no takers. Percy then designed a motorcycle that also failed to sell until it was offered as a more basic machine at 40 guineas and finally found a ready market. In 1911 Taylor became a British citizen and adopted Goodman as the family name and Veloce (Italian for fast) for all the family's motorcycles. Velocette (little Veloce, in essence) was adopted for the first lightweight in 1913. For the next few years Veloce continued to offer high-quality motorcycles that sold well, albeit with a reputation for being rather staid despite success in long distance trials.

By 1924 the family was hungry for road-racing success, enviously eyeing the achievements of rival factories' ohv engines. Percy set to work on his interpretation of such a 4-stroke single, constrained by the new engine having to be as narrow as possible to fit into Veloce's existing frames, which were designed for the less complex 2-stroke engines. But this proved to be a blessing as the narrow crankcase meant a short and strong crankshaft able to survive high revolutions, and Velocette's unique clutch inboard of the final-drive sprocket. The narrow crankcases also allowed the engine to sit low in the frame as a stressed member, aiding high speed handling. The

bore and stroke of 74 x 81mm would remain a constant for all 350cc ohc Velocettes. There was a 3-speed gearbox and, as on all Velocette singles, the primary drive was inboard of the final drive, so the engine sprocket is close to the drive-side main bearing, with minimal overhang. Like the narrow crankcase, this kept the engine small and strong.

The new model was debuted at the 1924 Olympia Show in London. Early failings were quickly addressed and it soon became apparent that Percy had designed something rather special. This was designated the K series, often said to celebrate the overhead 'Kamshaft', reflecting the family's German heritage, although the German for 'camshaft' is in fact Nockenwelle. It may in fact have been an excuse to make sure the K series happily followed the G and H Veloce models. The production racing version was the KSS (super sport).

Two of the new 350s were entered in the 1925 TT and, despite neither finishing, the Goodmans were happy with the overall performance of the motorcycles. They set their sights on Alec Bennett as a rider and team leader. This Irish-Canadian had come to England with the Canadian Army during World War I, serving as a despatch rider. His first TT was in 1921 with his first victory coming just a year later in the Senior. He would win five TTs between 1922 and 1928, riding in eighteen TT races and setting four lap records. In the 1924 Senior, Bennett became the first rider to win a race at over 60mph. Veloce announced that he would lead a team of three riders in the 1926 Junior TT, joined by Gus Kuhn and Fred Povey.

Bennett won the Junior TT by over 10 minutes, despite falling and cutting his chin en route to victory. With Kuhn and Povey in the top nine, Veloce also won the manufacturers' team prize. This was a remarkable success for such a tiny firm – at that time Veloce was still at its original, very small, Six Ways factory in Aston and had only forty-two employees. There was no racing department, the TT bikes being built by Percy and Eugene Goodman in the evenings. But the Goodmans were ambitious and in 1927 recruited racer, pilot and brilliant engineer Harold Willis.

1935 Velocette 348cc KTT Mk V. BONHAMS

THE GEARBOX OF THE FUTURE

For 1928 the works KSS was the motorcycle that introduced something that motorcyclists now take for granted: the positive-stop gear change. Before this riders had to change gear by hand, or tease a foot change into switching to a new ratio. Suddenly a rider could simply tap a gear lever, or block change through a number of gears, and would always find the gear lever in the same position, regardless of which ratio was engaged. The brainchild of Veloce's new designer Willis, this leap forwards helped Bennett to win that year's Junior TT by several minutes, followed home by Willis himself.

Veloce announced that a production version of Bennett's bike, the KTT ('Kamshaft' TT replica) would go on sale in 1929. The company had, by this time, realized that the Veloc-

ette name should be adopted across the entire range to reflect the public's love for the company's lightweights. The race the motorcycle was intended to compete in was given away by the nomenclature of the race-ready version: the Velocette KTT was born. This differed obviously from the road-going models such as the KSS by the external stiffening webs on the crankcase, inside which were lighter steel flywheels. The camshaft profile was also more extreme for more power at higher engine revolutions.

Demand for the new KTT was such that a decision was made to commit to expanded production and a new factory at Hall Green in south-east Birmingham, where Veloce would remain until their closure in February 1971. Each KTT was built by a single man, who would presumably know who he was assembling the motorcycle for. There was no production

21

In the 1928 Junior TT, Velocette's new 'positive stop' foot gear-change helped Alec Bennett to his fifth TT win and a new lap record of 61.19mph (108.13km/h), with his team mate Harold Willis second. TTRACEPICS.COM/IOMTT.COM

line, just perhaps dozen workstations producing a superb racing machine. This naturally made a KTT expensive, and would do so throughout production: in many years it cost an average man's annual wages.

Despite this the KTT soon became the default racing motorcycle for privateers. By the late 1930s it was the mainstay of the grids, going on to become one of the most successful 350cc production racing motorcycles of all time, notably in international competition. Partly this was because Velocette never rested on their laurels – the original was quickly designated the Mark I retrospectively, and each successive year's production was given a new Mark listing. For 1932 the Mark IV saw the coil valve-springs replaced by hairsprings, which from today's perspective might seem a backward step. But coil springs were still prone to breaking at the time, and hairsprings allowed better cooling of the valve stems and were reliable to a higher rpm limit. The Mark IV also made the previously optional 4-speed gearbox a standard fitting.

The next significant change came at the end of 1935 with the Mark V, which had a redesigned engine in a new full-cradle frame, keeping the engine low by placing the sump between the frame rails. During 1936 perhaps only six Mark VIs were built, now with the cast aluminium cylinder head from the KSS, including a 500cc version for the legendary Stanley

Woods. He took it to the first of three runner-up spots at the Senior TT, even his talent unable to defeat the speed of the Nortons.

The 1936 bike was a very special KTT, with a double overhead camshaft (dohc) head that preceded Norton's similar development by a year. Discouraged by camshaft drive snags, Willis did not pursue that development path. However, his ideas on rear suspension would be another ground-breaker. Velocette were only just beaten to fielding a racer with rear suspension by Moto Guzzi, whom Woods had previously ridden for. This was another leap forward by designer Harold Willis, who admired Dowty's oleo aircraft suspension. While Moto Guzzi had placed the springs for their rear suspension below the engine, this had inevitably meant raising the engine and centre of gravity. Willis positioned his air sprung 'Oleomatic' struts either side of the rear wheel, above the swing arm, effectively inventing the layout still in use today.

With Stanley Woods on board, Veloce were able to develop the KTT significantly for 1937's Mark VII. Moving the engine forward by around an inch and a half (40mm) improved handling and a barrel with much larger fins improved cooling, particularly as it was now less shrouded by the forks and front wheel, and so gave more power and reliability. While only thirty-seven of these KTTs were built they are considered

Note the number plate bracket – some people still ride the KTT on the road.

perhaps the most beautiful and successful of the Marks. The VI and VII have acquired near-mythical status, which is understandable given how few were built and how successful they were. The factory was to now focus on the high-camshaft ohv M series (which followed the K series!); this would be their mainstay both during and after the war.

THE REAR SUSPENSION OF THE FUTURE

Veloce put the Mark VIII, the first production motorcycle to use a swinging-arm rear fork with enclosed suspension above, on sale in 1938. This was effectively the previous year's works motorcycle, and turned the Junior TT into something of a Velocette benefit. Woods won followed home by team-mate Ted Mellor, leaving the works Nortons of Freddie Frith, John White and Harold Daniell to mop up the next three places. Beyond that, it was clear that a production Velocette was a match for the equivalent Norton.

The 1939 Junior TT was even more dramatic: of the thirty-five finishers, twenty-five were mounted on Velocettes including winner Stanley Woods. The Senior was perhaps more

impressive, given that privateers on Velocette 350s were up against 500cc machines. Thirteen of the thirty finishers were on Velocettes, although lead rider Woods could only manage fourth against Frith's Norton, itself been pushed down to third by the dominant supercharged BMW flat twins of Georg Meier and Jock West.

Harold Willis had anticipated serious competition from the BMW twins, although the Gilera Quattro (four) would beat them to the European championship. His response was a supercharged inline parallel twin with contra-rotating crankshafts to avoid the gyroscopic effect of the BMW flat twin that riders complained about. The design also avoided the ground clearance problems that BMW's layout introduced. Like the BMW, Willis's twin (which he named the Roarer) had shaft final dive that kept oil off the back tyre. Unlike the BMW's rather complex plunger rear suspension and exposed drive shaft, Willis enclosed the Velocette's shaft in a tube that doubled as a swinging arm, probably another first.

Stanley Woods rode the motorcycle in practice for the Senior TT and, although he was very positive about the design, elected to stick with the single for the race. This may have been to do with weight: the Roarer was a hefty 168kg (370lb), 20kg (44lb,) more than a standard KTT Mark VIII; both were heavier than the 137kg (302lb) BMW. The BMW was also more powerful – around 60bhp compared with the Roarer's 55bhp and a works 500cc KTT's 48bhp. But it showed that Willis and Velocette were still at the cutting edge of motorcycle design.

Sadly a shadow was cast over Velocette's achievements during the 1939 TT when director, designer and race chief Harold Willis died of meningitis following a simple medical procedure at the Nerve Hospital, Birmingham.

The big push to win the 1939 Senior TT by the German BMWs was of course the 'phoney war' in the run-up to the fires that burned throughout Europe for the following five years. There was little time for racing and certainly no TT. After the war the FIM decreed that superchargers were banned from racing and that a standard low-octane 'pool' petrol be used by all competitors. This was the first attempt to try to reduce the cost of going racing in a world that needed to rebuild, but also needed something to cheer about.

The TT resumed in 1947, Eugene's son Peter being almost the lone Velocette finisher in the Senior, in third place behind the works Nortons. The Junior TT was a much happier hunting ground, with the first four home on Velocettes: Bob Foster, David Whitworth, J.A. Weddell and Peter Goodman. The Mark VIII went back on sale, largely unchanged from 1938 and just about the only production racing motorcycle available to the general public.

The 1948 TT was less cheery, the best result for a Velocette in the Senior being a tenth for Eric Oliver. Oliver would be the first sidecar World Champion the following year, passengered by Denis Jenkinson. 'Jenks' went on to become one of the era's most famous motor sport reporters while Oliver won the sidecar championship a further three times.

In the 1948 Junior TT Freddie Frith won aboard Velocette followed home by team-mate Bob Foster. The next Velocette home was Oliver back in eighth, with the Nortons and rapidly improving AJS E90 'Porcupine' splitting them.

A NEW WORLD CHAMPIONSHIP

1949 brought the new World Championship, with 500cc the maximum capacity for the Blue Riband class, followed by 350, 250, 125cc classes for solos. There was also a 600cc sidecar class. The opening round was to be the Isle of Man TT, now also the British Grand Prix with the Duke of Edinburgh as the guest of honour. Velocette's team, sponsored and run by Dennis Mansell and Nigel Spring, decided that with Freddie Firth they had a realistic prospect in the 350 class. However, given

Freddie Frith and Velocette at Governors Bridge in the 1949 Junior TT. TTRACEPICS.COM/IOMTT.COM

that the KTT Mark VIII was a pre-war design, and that 1949 would be the final year of KTT production, more than a little fine tuning would be required.

A complete redesign of the valve gear was considered necessary, and Velocette's new chief designer Charles Udall had already trialled a twin-camshaft cylinder head on the works racers in 1936. The post-war revival, however, was the work of Bertie Goodman, only son of Percy who was by now the head of Veloce. Double overhead camshafts permit lighter and more precisely controlled valve gear, allowing a maximum of 8,000rpm as against the 7,200rpm limit applied to the sohc engines. The dohc 'double knocker' — a term first used by Harold Willis before the war — also had a raft of detail improvements over previous designs. These included machined-forged pistons and an exhaust valve filled with sodium to aid cooling. These post-war dohc engines were also fitted with bigger Oldham couplings in the vertical camshaft drive, and the camshafts and valve train were carefully balanced with counterweights to minimize vibration in the bevel drive. For the first time since before the war there was extensive use of Elektron magnesium alloy (including within the gearbox) and, as with most TT Grand Prix machines, larger-capacity fuel tanks. As with all TT bikes the oil filler was on the left side: in those days riders made pit stops on the east and nearside of the Glencrutchery Road, so their crew would be on the left as the motorcycle came in for refuelling and having the oil topped up. The opposite was more usually the case, as motorcycles were often leaned against a wall or fence for a rider to work on, the nearside of the road in Britain being on the left.

Veloce's racing team understood that both chassis and engine development had to go hand in hand. As with the original KSS, apart from a few teething problems, the dohc engine immediately offered an impressive power boost over the 'single-knockers' along with a much smoother power delivery. As with all the works racers, a much larger cylinder barrel improved cooling. Six such engines were built, some probably converted from single-camshaft motors.

With most of Veloce's finances allocated to developing the Velocette LE ('Little Engine', the 200cc flat twin 2-stroke beloved of police forces), post-war racing was funded by Castrol and dealers together with privateers Nigel Spring and R.S. (Dick) Wilkins. Spring paid for the use of Frith's KTT (frame number SF114 with engine number KTT 954) and team-mate Ken Bills' (SF129/KTT 956). The dohc motor was emphatically on loan: then, as today, factories did not want their rivals sharing their carefully garnered expertise. In an interview published in *Motor Cycling* early in 1948, Spring explained he had expected standard Mark VIII KTTs to be delivered, so 'was

delighted to hear that Veloce had decided to build a limited number of special models, with "hotted-up" engines'. In the same *Motor Cycling* article, Bertie Goodman confirmed that four of these special KTTs had been made: two for the Spring *équipe*, and one each for Bob Foster and David Whitworth.

Lead rider Frith was from Lincolnshire, a quiet, modest man, yet one of the few riders to win Isle of Man TTs before and after the war. First talent-spotted in 1930, when he finished third on a Velocette in the inaugural Junior Manx Grand Prix, in 1935 he won that race on a Norton, bagging him a ride on Veloce's works racer for 1936. He rewarded the factory with wins in the 1936 Junior TT and 1937 Senior TT, during which he became the first man to lap the Snaefell Course at over 90mph (145km/h). He spent the war years as a motorcycle instructor in the Army, tempted back to racing in 1947 at the age of thirty-eight. However, he did not race at the TT that year after a crash aboard a Moto Guzzi 500 single in practice for the Senior. He joined the Nigel Spring team for 1948, and set about making history.

FRITH AND VELOCETTE DOMINATE

Freddie Frith won five grands prix of the 1949 350cc World Championship season: the opening round at Isle of Man TT was followed by the Swiss (Bremgarten), Dutch (Assen) and Belgian (Spa Francorchamps) meetings. He then won the penultimate round, the Ulster Grand Prix at Clady, a 16-mile (26km) course of rough and narrow lanes. This was with a sohc motor (occasionally preferred for its better torque characteristics) and meant that Frith did not need to compete in final race of the season (the Nations Grand Prix at Monza), having already handsomely won the championship with the maximum possible points tally. Only a rider and manufacturer's best three results counted towards the final championship score, so once Frith and Velocette won at Spa Francorchamps in Belgium they were unbeatable.

Winning the 350cc class of the FIM's inaugural World Championship was the pinnacle of Freddie Frith's career and he subsequently retired, by then being forty years old. He was honoured with an OBE by King George VI at the end of the year for 'services to British motorcycle racing' in particular and 'British prestige' in general. Frith then opened a motorcycle dealership in Grimsby that traded successfully for many years. He died in 1988 aged seventy-eight and is still remembered fondly in Lincolnshire as one of the county's greatest sporting heroes.

THIS AND OPPOSITE PAGE: **Freddie Frith's 1949 world championship-winning, 1948 and
1949 Junior TT-winning, 1948 works Velocette 348cc dohc KTT.** BONHAMS

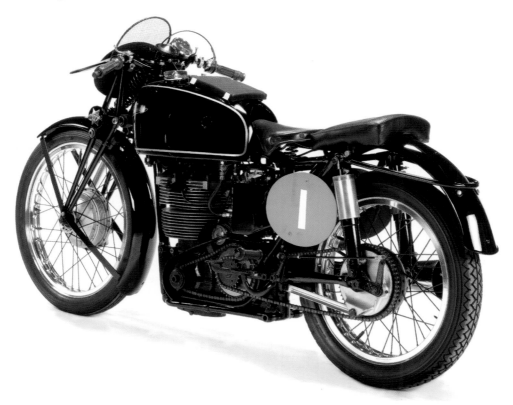

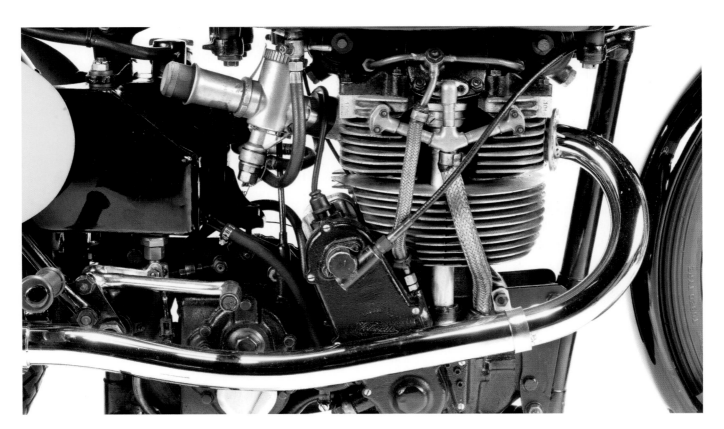

The drive side of the KTT hinted at the look of its pushrod successors.

Although Irishman Reg Armstrong's AJS took second place in the 1947 350cc World championship, with eighteen points to Frith's thirty-three (ten points for each win, plus an extra point for fastest lap), just two points behind Armstrong was Bob Foster, taking third place for Velocette. In the end, five of the ten classified finishers in the championship were on Velocettes, including Ernie Lyons in eighth and also ninth for Velocette in the 500 class.

The exceedingly fast dohc 350s raced on into 1950, Bob Foster winning the World Championship for Velocette for the second year in succession. But by now the Manx Norton was stretching its legs, aided by Norton's far bigger budget and new star Geoff Duke. From 1946 the Manx had gained new telescopic forks and, while Veloce responded by developing a new lightweight 'lowboy' frame for 1951, the girder forks remained. Once again raced by Foster (now in his final year), as well as new team members Cecil Sandford and Bill Lomas, this would turn out to be the swansong for the full Velocette race team in international events, and the race shop was closed down soon afterwards. For 1952 Veloce only entered a single rider, the first 500cc World Champion Les Graham, who failed to finish the Junior TT and was joint last in the 350 World Championship. Not only were Norton looking to be back to their pre-war unbeatable self, a new rising star from AJS, the 7R, was clearly more than a match for the Velocette KTT.

THE BEGINNING OF THE END

Another factor in the company's decision to close the racing department was the death after an illness in 1952 of the chief race designer and company principal, Peter Goodman. He had been working on a new 4-cylinder, water-cooled, racing engine that was – as usual with Velocettes – ahead of its time, but the project died with him. The factory did build a 250cc version of the KTT but it was too heavy to offer a serious threat to the fast-emerging competition. Therefore, 1952 marked the end of the road for the KTT racer, with numbers fast reducing in the following years as more affordable and competitive race machinery became available, especially from Norton and AJS.

Perhaps wisely, Velocette switched focus to the ohv 500 singles, achieving remarkable success in showrooms, at clubman racing and record setting. But for the purist, such machines can never have the appeal of a Grand Prix racing motorcycle, and the KTT continued to be a reasonable mount for amateur racers. As late as 1958 Harry Hinton Junior entered a dohc Velocette at Sachsenring for the German Grand Prix, taking a creditable fifth in class.

Production of the Velocette Mark VIII KTT ended in 1949 (or perhaps early 1950), with some 238 examples built: 49 before the war and a further 189 after. While numbers of the

1935 Velocette 348cc
KTT MkV. BONHAMS

The pushrod singles that replaced the KTT have probably an even greater following.

works engine are not known for certain, it is thought that just six machines were assembled in the post-war period. Velocette ceased developing machines for Grand Prix racing almost as soon as their initial success in the nascent World Championship, presumably expecting Peter Goodman's 4-cylinder racer to take on the dohc KTT's mantle.

So Velocette's racing success in the future came with modified road-going machinery, due mainly to the high cost of competing at the highest level. The M series ohv single that had been launched in 1935 – developed with the expectation that most owners would add a sidecar – resumed production in 1954. For 1955 it was relaunched in a far sportier vein as the Venom, which would eventually become the Thruxton in 1965.

Even though the Venom and Thruxton still have a huge fan base, their pushrod ohv layout was far less exotic than the bevel-driven ohc layout of the KTT. But the overhead cam was just too costly to build, and far more difficult to assemble and rebuild, than a pushrod ohv single. The switch was undoubtedly the right thing for Velocette to do, as their competition became 2-cylinder motorcycles that could stretch beyond 500cc in a marketplace where the mantra was very much becoming 'bigger is better'. This came to apply to the number of cylinders as well as to capacity, and eventually left Velocette painted into a corner even before the Japanese started to make inroads into customers' hearts and minds that the British motorcycle factories had assumed were theirs by right. Yet in their heyday the KTTs were unbeatable, and they are still rightly revered.

CHAPTER FOUR

MANX NORTON

It is a fair wager that if you asked even a non-motorcyclist to name a motorcycle the Manx Norton would be close to the top of the list of names people remember. Part of that would be down to Geoff Duke's achievements on the bike as he was practically royalty to a certain generation. Yet the bike was named almost by accident, initially simply the racing version of Norton's International 500 single. The nascent motorcycles came down the production line either tagged 'Inter' for the road-going models or 'Manx' for the racers. The Manx name was soon taken up by everyone, perhaps oddly as a prefix: all other model names across motorcycling come after the marque's name. So while the first motorcycle from the factory was the Norton Energette and the last the Norton Commando, in between them came the uniquely named Manx Norton. Nobody seems to know why.

James Lansdowne 'Pa' Norton founded his eponymous business in 1898, as a manufacturer of 'fittings and parts for the two-wheel trade'. In late 1902 the first complete Norton motorcycles were offered, with French and Swiss engines. But the big break came in 1907 when Harry Rem-

This 1947 Manx Norton was purchased by the film star Maureen O'Hara for her brother, Jimmy FitzSimons, for his twenty-first birthday in 1947. BONHAMS

Trucked over to the Isle of Man, but the number plate means it can be ridden on the road.

brandt 'Rem' Fowler won the Isle of Man 2-cylinder class riding a Norton with a 700cc Peugeot V-twin motor, although he was beaten by the Matchless that won the single-cylinder class.

This was the beginning of a strong racing tradition for Norton. Success in the very first Isle of Man TT race, followed by wins at Brooklands and other European races, helped cement Norton's reputation as a builder of serious road and race bikes. In 1908 the company offered their first engine built in-house, a single-cylinder side-valve unit, and by 1909 they were on sale in Harrods.

The famous cursive Norton logo, still in use today, was laid out by Pa Norton and his daughter Ethel, first on the front of their 1914 catalogue and by 1916 on the motorcycle's fuel tanks. Recovering from a 1912 bankruptcy, the new owners recognized that Pa, despite his poor health, was a man of vision and central to the success of the Norton factory. He died aged just fifty-six in 1925, but not before he had seen his motorcycles win the Senior and Sidecar TTs in 1924, with the 500cc Model 18, Norton's first ohv single.

But, presumably inspired by Velocette's new KSS/TT, a new ohc Norton motor was penned by Walter Moore over the winter of 1926–27. The 79 – 100mm (a slightly larger ratio of bore to stroke than the Velocette) would remain almost unchanged on Norton's 500 racing singles until 1953. Stanley Woods tested the new prototype in Germany in early 1927, but it broke down. The use of bevels for the camshaft drive never changed despite teeth breaking on early models, an issue that never completely went away. Ironically Mike Hailwood's 1978 TT-winning Ducati suffered the same problem, fortunately after he crossed the finishing line.

The new Norton's bottom end was based on the existing Model 18 that has gone into production in 1922, but otherwise the design was all new. The top set of bevel gears was enclosed by an aluminium cambox and the magneto for the ignition was placed above the back of the crankcase, just in front of a new 3-speed foot-change gearbox. Above this was the oil tank, a wraparound design on the racers so that the filler could be on the right or, for TT racing, on the left as on the Velocette. Stanley Woods joked that Moore had both a

A left-hand oil tank filler is a TT racing option, because pit stop crews serviced the bike from that side. Until comparatively recently riders made pit stops on the east (nearside) of the Glencrutchery Road, so their crew would be on the left as the motorcycle came in for refuelling and having the oil topped up.

Velocette and a Charter Lea (with a Blackburne single converted to ohc) in his office and probably copied the worst features of both. However, the Oldham couplings in the valve-gear drive-train remained a feature on the 'cammy Nortons', as they did on the Velocette.

THE FIRST WIN

The 1927 Senior TT was the first of many wins for the 'Manx'. For 1928, the CS1 (Cam Shaft [model] 1) was offered at £89 (when the average man's weekly wage was about £5) for riders who wanted to go racing or just own a fine sporting motorcycle. During that year's Isle of Man TT the CJ (Camshaft Junior), a 71 x 88mm 350, was trialled but found uncompetitive. The 500 was also increasingly beset by problems, contributing to designer Moore leaving Norton for NSU – and, it was said, for more money. He would continue to evolve his design for the German factory, leading to the parry that NSU stood

for 'Norton Spares Used', rather than as an abbreviation of Neckarsulm, the city where NSU was based.

The rights to Moore's design were his own, rather than Norton's, so this settled the need for a complete redesign. Arthur Carroll took over Moore's role, working with Edgar Franks and Norton rider/development engineer Joe Craig; Craig was a gifted racer with wins for Norton including in his native Ulster. The team debuted the now-famous 'Carroll' engine at the North West 200 in Northern Ireland in spring 1930. Despite extensive changes the original bore and stroke were retained, but sadly, unlike Moore's design, the cambox was never oil-tight, with openings for the rocker arms. Elsewhere the design owed even more to the Velocette KTT motor, down to the new Oldham couplings in the camshaft dive. This chassis was also original, a new cradle frame with Webb girder forks, and front and rear 8-inch brakes. But the easiest way to identify one of Carroll's engines is the downdraft angle of the carburettor, rather than a horizontal inlet that Moore specified. Initially carrying over the CS1 and CJ designations,

Oil tank fillers were usually on the right for British road bikes, to facilitate filling up while leaned against a wall, the nearside of the road in Britain being on the left.

the International name replaced them in 1932, the Model 30 being the 500 and Model 40 the 350. However, as we have already seen, the racing versions were soon dubbed the Manx Norton, even if the name was not officially applied until 1947.

EVOLUTION NOT REVOLUTION

At the very highest level the new CS1 'Manx' struggled to match the four-valve Rudge but was quickly recognized as a motorcycle that was available over the counter yet was competitive in international events – hence the official designation. As with the Velocette KTT, development was evolutionary rather than revolutionary. Hairspring valve control replaced the coil springs, fuel and oil capacities increased and the works bikes gained plunger rear suspension to replace the rigid rear frame: this was the famous 'garden gate' design, and was

eventually made available to privateers. The engines became ever closer to square, the 500 initially gaining an extra 0.7mm on the bore in 1936 to make it the full 499cc permitted by the FIM and the Model 40 bore and stroke became 73.4 x 82.5mm (349cc). In 1938 a further revision made the Model 30 82 x 92.3mm and the Model 40 75.9 x 77mm. With an 11:1 compression ratio and running on a petrol–benzole mix, the 500 gave 52bhp at 6,500rpm – good enough for 120mph.

A bigger cylinder head gave the necessary increase in cooling, another indication of Joe Craig's careful programme of improvements rather than a complete redesign, let alone more cylinders. When Sturmey Archer ceased production of the gearbox Norton used they bought the rights and had them built by Burman, improving the positive stop mechanism. The 4-speed cluster was to be used throughout Norton's history, almost the same unit being fitted to the 1970s Commandos. The big leap forward was the dohc heads for the works bikes, first tried in practice for the 1937 TT and offered to customers on production racers from 1949. Telescopic forks, albe-

Geoff Duke flies down Bray Hill in the 1950 Senior TT. TTRACEPICS.COM

it undamped, were adopted pre-war (possibly copied from BMW's units) and catalogued for 1940 – but of course never produced.

Between the wars Norton won the Isle of Man Senior TT race ten times and, between 1930 and 1937, won seventy-eight of ninety-two Grand Prix races. But with war clouds gathering Norton looked towards the needs of the military rather than racers. Almost inevitably this meant losing racing enthusiast Joe Craig who, in January 1939, left Norton to join BSA.

Norton management was, however proved right. In the 1930s they were selling perhaps 4,000 motorcycles a year but between 1937 and 1945 built almost 100,000 side-valve motorcycles for the military. When racing resumed after the war Norton, like the other British single-cylinder racers, found that the ban on supercharging and the requirement to race on 70 octane 'pool petrol' favoured their finely developed motorcycles rather better than the multi-cylinder opposition, initially at least. Norton had to do little beyond

drop the Manx's compression ration from 11 to 7:1 while the Italian fours and the AJS Porcupine twin had to be re-designed to run without superchargers, a bigger task than might be imagined: an inlet tract that is designed to have fuel and air pushed rather than sucked into it has a different set of design parameters.

ANOTHER WIN, BUT JUST THE ONE

Even so Harold Daniell's Senior TT win was the only classic victory for Norton in 1946, a remarkable achievement given that he had last won the Senior TT in 1938, also for Norton. This from a man who had been denied active wartime service on account of his poor eyesight! Yet Norton's 1949 win was hardly a comfort given that Les Graham's AJS 2-cylinder 'Porcupine' started the last lap with a 90-second advantage. Sadly for Graham – but luckily for Norton – the AJS sheared its magneto drive with three miles to go. Graham pushed in from Hillberry to eventually cross the line in tenth place. So Daniell was the winner, with Norton team-mate Johnny Lockett second and Velocette-mounted Ernie Lyons third.

But away from the Isle of Man, Norton struggled. The British didn't necessarily build the best motorcycles, but they had the riders who knew the Isle of Man's 37-and-a-bit miles better than anyone else. The course has always taken years to learn, certainly before a rider can challenge for a win and, although the TT has always attracted international entries (including from as far afield as Egypt in the 1930s), it was riders from the British Isles who came back year after year. The other circuits

used for the new World Championship were a test of power and bravery as much as knowing which way the road went next. Yet even here, while the Manx was the favoured choice of the midfield rider, Triumph twins and even Velocette 350s were giving the Norton a run for its money.

And then there was Joe Craig, returned to the Norton fold. His factory squad was a slick TT-winning machine, with an unrivalled signalling team around the course. They also had the fastest bikes and could cherry pick the best riders, for now at least. Critics were predicting the end of an era as the Italian fours improved and Norton would be unable to compete with motorcycles with perhaps 30 per cent more power. Indeed Norton started drawing up plans for their own four, even more radical than the Italians'.

Peter Duke with his father's 1950s works Manx Norton. MANXNORTON.CO.NZ/IOMTT.COM

For its time – work on the project was abandoned in 1953 – the Norton four had features not seen on the post-war competition including water cooling, forward-facing carburettors and exhaust ports at the rear. A complete engine was built and tested on a dynamometer. So certain was Norton that this was their future that Joe Craig handed over the racing team to Steve Lancefield while he spent a year on secondment with the BRM racing team, to better understand 4-cylinder racing engines. Only a miracle could save the Manx single from oblivion.

THE FEATHERBED AND GEOFF DUKE ARRIVE

And then came not one, but two miracles. A completely new frame that would be the inspiration for almost all mainstream motorcycles frames until Antonio Cobas invented the beam frame first adopted by Yamaha. It was the work of Rex Mc-Candless, a successful former motorcycle racer and designer from Northern Ireland. During the war he had worked in aviation, subsequently working as a vehicle mechanic until, in

Michael Russell and the Works Izzard Manx Norton at Ginger Hall during the 2017 Bennetts Senior Classic TT race. IOMTT.COM/DAVE KNEEN/PACEMAKER PRESS

1943, going into business with his brother Cromie to repair vehicles for the Ministry of Supply. It was at this time that he built his own motorcycle, which became the prototype for the successful featherbed frame adopted by the Norton Motorcycle Company.

Harold Daniell gave the frame its name after his first test ride, saying it was so easy to ride fast that it was like 'riding on a featherbed' because it could be more softly sprung than the 'garden gate' plunger frame – and the name stuck. Mc-Candless was also one of the first to recognize the worth of

smaller wheel sizes (making a motorcycle more manoeuvrable, especially at speed) and specified 19-inch wheels rather than the garden gate's 21-inch items. The twin cradle loop that form the main frame and the swinging arm look unexceptional to us now, but that's because the layout became so widely adopted as to become ubiquitous, McCandless' genius hiding in plain sight.

Norton's miracle number two was signing up a young Geoff Duke. He had made his racing debut in 1948 in the Junior TT on a 350cc Norton borrowed from the works team. His en-

BELOW AND RIGHT: **Norton Model 40, c. 1957.** BONHAMS

gine failed due to a split oil tank but his performance – he led the race at the end of lap three – impressed observers and he was marked as a star of the future. His first road-racing victory was when he beat Les Graham in the 350cc final at Haddenham in 1949. He won the Senior Manx Grand Prix later that year, as well as the Senior Clubman's TT.

Duke was that rarest of racers, blindingly fast and just relying on natural talent but also a tremendous development rider, able to understand how he might ride any given motorcycle even faster. The most obvious example of this was his first gift to motorcycling: one piece leathers. His idea seems obvious for racing now, a lightweight, close-fitting suit with minimal pockets and padding rather than the weighty and bulky two piece outfits of yore. He approached Frank Barker, a tailor in St Helens, Merseyside, to make him a bespoke aerodynamic leather outfit. Barker measured his client crouching over a chair as if riding a motorcycle. The finished suit weighed a little over 2kg (5lb) and was ready for the 1950 Senior TT.

Duke won that race wearing his new leathers for the first time and would have romped away with the championship had he not had problems with delaminating tyres. Duke would go on to be World Champion three times for Norton, winning two 350cc titles in 1951 and 1952 and the 500cc title in 1951. No wonder they forgot about the four! And it wasn't just Duke who made the Manx fly: in the 1950 Senior TT the first eleven home were all on Nortons bar Graham on the AJS in fourth and Reg Armstrong in sixth on a Velocette. The Model 40 was almost as dominant in the Junior TT. Here was a motorcycle built on a production line and sold alongside the road bikes at Norton dealers that was capable of winning a TT in the right hands, and of bringing a young rider to the attention of a factory racing team.

It wasn't very different on the world stage. Duke just missed out on the 1950 500cc title, his two retirements gifting Gilera's Umberto Masetti the championship despite Duke's three wins to Masetti's two. If you couldn't get a works ride, a Manx Norton was now the best bike racing motorcycle you could buy. With race organizers paying start money it was just about possible to live hand to mouth in the Blue Riband class of the continental circus and FIM World Championship if you bought a Manx – that would remain the case well into the 1960s and arguably even later. Certainly there was nothing that had such an impact on the ability of privateers to compete at the highest level until the arrival of the Yamaha 2-stroke 350 twins around 1970.

NEW LAP RECORDS

In 1950 the TT also said goodbye to pool petrol, immediately allowing record laps in all three classes. Duke and the factory Manx ran away with the show: he stole all the headlines by leading his first ever Senior TT throughout the seven laps, destroying race and lap records. Bar Bill Doran in runner-up spot on the Porcupine, the top fourteen riders were all on board a Manx.

Earlier in the week Duke had become the first rider of a Junior machine to lap the mountain course at over 90mph (145km/h). Once again he led from start to finish and, on his second lap, he established a new record of 91.38mph (147.03km/h). He also won the 350 and 500 World Championships for Norton, despite the ambitions of the Italian factories. The many privateers in the midfield also won Norton the constructor's championship.

In 1952, twenty-nine of the forty-one motorcycles to finish the Senior TT would be Manx Nortons. Duke repeated his 350 World Championship win for Norton that year, his focus only interrupted by a spell racing cars. At the suggestion of English aviation pioneer and Conservative politician Lord Brabazon he tried his hand at racing on four wheels for the year. Brabazon arranged a test with Aston Martin and John Wyer, the firm's racing manager, considered that Duke had 'great potential'. Duke drove a DB3 to take third place in the Goodwood Easter Monday Race in 1952 and the following year took a works Aston Martin to the 12 Hours of Sebring endurance race in Florida; he was teamed with Peter Collins, though they crashed and failed to finish. In the summer of 1953 Duke again committed fully to motorcycles, moving to the faster 4-cylinder racers of the Italian manufacturer Gilera. Despite this, Rhodesian Ray Amm brought home the double for Norton once again at the 1953 TT, with wins in the Senior and Junior TTs. While the AJS 7R was making inroads into Norton's customer base in the 350 class, the 500 Norton was still the bike to own.

The World Championship was, however, a different matter. Duke led a Gilera one–two–three finish in the 500 class and Moto Guzzi's brilliant horizontal single was starting its reign in the 350 championship. Therefore, 1954 saw a substantial redesign of the Norton single. The 30M was now oversquare for the first time at 86 x 85.62mm (499cc) and the 40M almost so at 76 x 76.7mm (348cc), the works bikes having had these engines since 1952. Before the works effort ceased (at the end of the 1955 season) the factory 500s went oversquare, at 88 x 82mm, although these dimensions were never offered over the counter. The barrel and bevel drive assemblies were tidied up and there was a steeper inlet tract. This might sound like a major overhaul, but in fact it was half-hearted compared

An original Manx: compare this with the modern racing replica.

One of the modern replica Manxes built for classic racing, including at the **Manx Grand Prix** and **Classic TT.**

with what was planned and the result of Norton's decision to abandon the World Championship and focus on selling the Manx to privateers, while offering more limited support to riders felt to have a future.

The Manx did win the 1954 Senior TT, albeit under controversial circumstances. The race had been delayed by 30 minutes by horrendous weather conditions, but when it did get started Ray Amm and his Norton seemed completely oblivious to the conditions and was soon running with a good minute in hand over second-placed Duke on the Gilera Quattro. When race was shortened from six laps to four after Duke had stopped for fuel and Amm had ridden straight on, Giuseppe Gilera protested to the ACU that the Norton team must have been tipped off. The controversy was such that the FIM excluded the results from the World Championship. The truth is difficult to be sure of: Amm was faster than Duke and the Norton used less fuel, and he might have been planning a splash and dash.

JOHN SURTEES AND THE MYSTERIOUS FLAT SINGLE

One of the riders Norton would support in 1955 was a young John Surtees, but he was warned that Norton would only enter a limited number of races and that the bikes would

be 'works development' Manxes – testbeds for the factory's customer production racing models. Norton offered Surtees £500 as a down payment, about half a year's salary. But what drew in Surtees were the rumours of the prototype F-model Manx. It was ultimately never mentioned, let alone raced, but Surtees did track down what was left of the model.

Norton's policy by this time was to stick to just one cylinder with its works machines, although there were still things that the factory's race chief Joe Craig could do. This was his latest prototype, the cylinder tipped forward to lower the bike's centre of gravity, benefit from down-draught carburation and provide better airflow to the engine with a dustbin fairing. Moto Guzzi was already demonstrating how effective a streamlined horizontal single could be by dominating the 350cc World Championship. Also, like the Moto Guzzi and some factory Manxes, the Norton Model F (for flat single) had an external flywheel to minimize oil drag. There was an innovative 5-speed gearbox that, like much of the engine, was designed to be as small as possible. The Italians had long tried to keep their racing motorcycles as compact as they could be, but such attention to packaging was a leap forward for British racing motorcycles. The proposed dustbin fairing would add 10–12mph to the top speed. Pannier fuel tanks were an option and, like the low headstock, kept the centre of gravity low and the frontal area small. And the main frame members ran from the headstock straight towards the rear of the unit-construction motor. This was revolutionary in Britain.

The prototype flat single (Model F) designed to extend the competitive life of the Manx. This is the 350 version.

Bruce Anstey on the McIntosh replica Norton at Quarterbridge. IOMTT.COM/DAVE KNEEN/PACEMAKER PRESS

The trailing link forks hinted at Norton's intention to use a dustbin fairing, offering stability under braking and better airflow to the cylinder head. Norton's Ray Amm and mechanic Charlie Edwards tested the bike at the MIRA test track in October 1954, without a fairing, and were delighted with the potential. But Norton and the Associated Motor Cycles Group (AMC, who owned AJS and Matchless) instead both agreed to pull out of World Championship racing. Amm departed for MV Agusta and Edwards was told to dismantle the prototype F-type and find somewhere to hide it away in Norton's Bracebridge Street factory. Years later it would be rescued and restored by Surtees, and there is a 350 version in Sammy Miller's museum.

Norton's management, in erasing the project, confirmed that they should be racing motorcycles that reflected what they were selling. But their top-of-the-range Dominator was a twin and their road-going 500 singles really bore no relationship to the Manx. In truth motorcycle sales were in decline, especially those built for sidecars. The first sidecar World Championship winner was powered by a 600cc version of the Manx, but new cars were becoming increasingly affordable for families and tradesmen. The Fiat 500 Nuova would arrive in 1957, hitting motorcycle sales hard and precipitating the withdrawal of the Italian factories from Grand Prix racing as they attempted to rein in expenditure, although MV Agusta would have an infamous change of heart.

The Italians, like Norton, were very much now ruled by accountants who put sales and profitably ahead of prestige and racing for the sake of the sport, and would henceforth only support a chosen few riders. Development of the Manx would reflect this for the remainder of its life and, in fairness,

with the premier World Championship seemingly run over the next few decades for the benefit of Count Agusta's ego, it is difficult to believe another course would have benefitted Norton beyond the short term.

Gilera would provide the only competition to MV Agusta in the premier class until their withdrawal from racing at the end of 1957. Their 4-cylinder racer dominated the 1953 500cc World Championship, taking the first three places led by Duke. But the opening round – the Senior TT – was a Norton one–two by Ray Amm and Jack Brett. Duke's team-mate Reg Armstrong was third, but his was the only 4-cylinder machine to cross the line – the other Gilera 500s and all the MV Agustas failed to finish. The Isle of Man's bumps and long sections that were taken flat-out were unforgiving mistresses; the Norton's rugged and (comparative) simplicity was still a huge advantage on the mountain course.

It also looked like the motorcycles Norton had in the showrooms. Gilera would often race their big single, the 499cc Saturno, in Italian events where their Quattro might have been expected to fare better. But Gilera knew they had to promote the bikes on sale as well as just the brand. Although Norton had launched the 497cc Model 7 in 1949 – their first twin, designed by Bert Hopwood – the rest of the range was single-cylinder models. The Model 7 and the singles were mainly thought of as sidecar-pullers until the 1952 Dominator 88 that brought the famous featherbed frame to the twins, previously not offered precisely because it was not simple to fit a sidecar to the design.

The final trauma for Norton's racing department was investors' concern over the future of motorcycling and the UK's troubled economy. AMC mopped up the shares and it proved to be a wise move. Although motorcycle sales went through a recession, more generally in the 1950s western economies were improving. While those who just needed transport turned to cars, true motorcycle enthusiasts, especially in the United States, were turning to large-capacity 2-cylinder motorcycles with a sporting bent. Norton sales flourished because, as a small manufacturer compared with Triumph and especially BSA, a little growth in the motorcycle market overall meant big numbers to Norton. The Dominator twin was enlarged to first 597cc, then 646cc (the 1961 Manxman/650SS) and finally to 745cc (the 1962 Atlas) which kept sales buoyant, especially in the United States.

THE DOMINATOR THAT DIDN'T

As might be expected, Norton developed the Dominator for racing but it remained outclassed by the Manx. The design had been determined by a need for robustness with iron barrels and heads, the pushrod-driven overhead valves limiting how high the motor could rev. The highly developed 500cc Dominator engine intended as a racing successor to the Manx produced 55bhp – barely more than the Manx was now making

– and revved to 8,000rpm. The overall weight was 35lb (16kg) less than a Manx when mounted in a special lightweight 'low-boy' frame to create the factory's Domiracer.

In the 1961 TT Tom Phillis took a Domiracer to third place and lapped at over 100mph (160km/h), a first for a pushrod engine and a first for any twin. The scale of that achievement is underlined by the fact that the only people who beat him were Mike Hailwood and Bob McIntyre (the first man to lap the mountain course at over 100mph), both riding Manx Nortons. Indeed, apart from a brace of 2-cylinder Matchless G45s, the top fourteen finishers were all Norton-mounted.

Norton abandoned the Domiracer project in 1962 when the Bracebridge Street race shop closed. The Domiracer and factory spares were sold to Paul Dunstall, who continued with development and began producing Norton performance parts.

It was not hard to see why. Apart from the rise of the AJS 7R 350 (like the Norton an AMC product, of course) in the Junior TT, the Manx remained as fast as anything bar the Italian fours across the mountain course. The 1961 result was something of an aberration: with John Surtees switching to cars, Count Agusta took a year out to cherry pick his next rider. Gary Hocking was allowed the run the previous year's bikes under a Privat banner and won every round he finished, only failing at the Nations (Italian) and both Isle of Man rounds, gifting Phil Read the Junior aboard a Norton. It wasn't long

Jamie Coward (500 Norton Ted Woof Craven Manx Norton) in Kirk Michael during a qualifying session for the Bennett's Classic TT.
IOMTT.COM/DAVE KNEEN/ PACEMAKER PRESS

This plunger-framed Norton single was being used as a pit bike.

before Mike Hailwood received a call from the Count, and normal service by the dominant MV Agusta team was soon resumed.

The final and most significant change to the 1957 Manxes was that the bevels were redesigned with a coarser pitch. As power and revs increased the finer type of bevel would break, especially with the 90mm bore machines (78.4mm stroke), which were based on Craig's 1954 engines but with internal flywheels. These were designed by Doug Hele who had re-joined Norton along with Bert Hopwood, the designer of the 2-cylinder Dominator engine.

Even so, in theory the Manx was obsolete and lacking in development as the 1960s dawned, yet it would still pulled rabbits out of the hat. Hailwood was second in the 1961 500 World Championship, having started the season with a Norton, and the next four places were filled by Manx pilots. However, this was to be the final season the Manx was of-fered, although a few were built up subsequently. In July 1962 AMC announced that Norton would be moving from its Bracebridge Street home to the AMC (AJS and Matchless) factory in Woolwich, London. It is understandable that from then on AMC focused on the Matchless G45 and G50 single,

although forty-two Manx Nortons were assembled between November 1962 and January 1963. Yet to call the motorcy-cle uncompetitive was hardly fair: Phil Read was third in the 1962 championship with a Manx and Jack Ahearn took one to runner-up spot in 1964, behind Hailwood and the MV. Almost unbelievably, Godfrey Nash took a Manx to third in the 500cc World Championship in 1969, although most riders had re-alized its days were numbered. When Nash rode a Norton Manx to the win at the 1969 Yugoslavian Grand Prix at the Opatija circuit, it would be the last time that a single-cylinder motorcycle was victorious in a 500 Grand Prix.

On the Isle of Man, Derek Minter took a Manx to the run-ner-up spot in the 1964 Senior TT, beaten by Hailwood's MV Agusta but ahead of the Matchless G45s that AMC seemed to be more interested in. The 1965 Senior TT had a near-iden-tical result bar Joe Dunphy being on the Norton. A Manx made it onto the podium in each of the next three Senior TTs, but that was really a swansong. Even so, that made the Manx a competitive privateer's mount during four decades, and presumably towards the end it was being raced by people who hadn't been born when this remarkable motorcycle first turned a wheel in anger.

CHAPTER FIVE

AJS PORCUPINE

AJS motorcycles can trace its history back to blacksmith Joseph Stevens (Joe to family and friends) and his sons Joseph (also a Joe in practice) and Harry's first engine in 1897. They had already been selling complete motorcycles with American Mitchell 4-stroke singles and – rightly – felt they could do better themselves. In short order this led to the Stevens Motor Manufacturing Company of Wolverhampton offering motorcycles for sale. By 1905 the Stevens were selling a model with a JAP (John Alfred Prestwich) V-twin engine, leading-link front forks and a swinging arm at the rear, something that AJS would be one of the first to develop into what we would recognize today as rear suspension.

In 1909 the company morphed into AJS to take on board more Stevens brothers, George and Albert John, known as Jack. While it was Albert John Stevens who lent his initials to the company – possibly because he was the eldest of the brothers involved in the business – it was very much a family concern. To pick an instance, in 1922 Harry was managing director and George the commercial manager, Joe Junior ran the experimental section and Jack worked as the production manager.

Their first 125cc engines were built to sell to other companies. In 1910 the first AJS was a 292cc, 2.5HP, single with options of either direct belt drive or a two-speed gearbox with chain drive.

Les Graham and the AJS Porcupine in the 1950 Senior TT. The near-horizontal cylinders identify this as the original E90 model. TTRACEPICS.COM

The 45-degree inclined cylinders identify this (and all subsequent images) as of the later E95 version. BONHAMS

The early adoption of a form of gearbox would be crucial to AJS's first visit to the Isle of Man in 1911, the first year that the motorcycles were expected to climb Snaefell. Little did the 104 riders who entered the TT realize what a challenge the new mountain course would be. The 7-mile climb from Ramsey to the Bungalow would bring with it a need for ingenuity. Single-gear machines seemed out of the question if the mountain was to be conquered, although just under a third of the motorcycles entered were so equipped. Indian and Scott were already using chain drive, and Triumph fitted a 3-speed Sturmey Archer hub gear similar to that on older bicycles. Matchless had a 6-speed belt-drive arrangement, but it was AJS's 3-speed gearbox that was arguably closer to what we are used to today than anything else on the Island.

For the first time the TT was split into two separate races (as opposed to classes), the four-lap Junior event allowing 300cc singles and 340cc twins, with 500cc singles and 585cc twins racing in the five-lap Senior. The course measured 37½ miles (60km), about a quarter of a mile shorter than the current Mountain Course, the difference being that riders turned right at Cronk-ny-Mona, instead of left towards Signpost, reaching the top of Bray Hill via Willaston. The start was down on the Quarterbridge Road, with refuelling depots at Braddan and Ramsey.

AJS had a fair first TT, its riders J.D. Corke and Jack Stevens both finishing the Junior in fourteenth and fifteenth places, respectively. AJS stayed away in 1912, partly because they couldn't keep up with demand for their motorcycles, but many manufacturers had anyway agreed to boycott the 1912 races, citing the difficulty of the new mountain course. But when AJS did return in 1914 it would be triumphant. Riding the new 2¾HP AJS, Eric Williams won the Junior TT at a record average speed of 45.58mph (73.34km/h). He was followed home by fellow AJS team member Cyril Williams in second place, with the rest of the team all finishing, taking fourth, sixth and twenty-ninth. The team and factory was feted as local heroes on their return home. Sales boomed and a die was cast: AJS was about racing, especially at the TT.

In 1921 (little of relevance to this story having happened since 1914 due to World War I) Howard Davies, on an ohv 350 AJS, became to first rider to win both the Senior and Junior TT on the same machine, a feat that has never been repeated. The company went from strength to strength, even building cars but, as with so many, the arrival of the 1930s brought financial crisis to AJS. During 1931 AJS was wound up, creditors paid in full and the rights sold to Matchless via a takeover by AMC. The Stevens brothers remained owners of the Retreat Street Works and continued as an engineering business. The car business was sold to Willys Overland Crossley, but few cars were produced.

To the Collier brothers' credit AJS wasn't simply subsumed into Matchless, although the factory was moved to their London base. By 1934 its racing success was recognized and rebooted, principally with the ohc 350 that had been designed by the Stevenses prior to the sale of AJS. Top-ten finishes in the Junior TT followed, but by the end of the decade racing was abandoned by AMC as the clouds of war gathered.

The classic black and gold paintwork mimicked the AJS 7R rather than the silver of the E90. BONHAMS

THE FIRST PLANS FOR A RACING TWIN

Joe Craig, as we have seen, left Norton shortly before World War II when Norton withdrew from racing – Craig's first love. After a spell at BSA he landed at AMC in 1939 and set about persuading the owners – the Collier brothers – that a new 2-cylinder racer was the future. They already had a fast but fragile AJS V4, but Craig was very much of the 'to finish first, first you must finish' school of racing. The liquid-cooled four might have allowed Walter Rusk to become the first rider to lap at the Ulster Grand Prix at over 100mph in August 1939, but even that achievement was marred with a DNF ('Did Not Finish') when a girder fork snapped. In truth, the V4 was no faster than the simpler Gilera inline four, and handled even more poorly. Although AJS had shown a road-going version of the V4 at Olympia in 1935, Harry Collier realized

that they were adding weight and complexity faster than they were reducing lap times

The Collier brothers, who had merged AJS, Matchless and Sunbeam into Associated Motor Cycles (AMC) in 1938, had themselves been TT winners. They realized there must be a compromise and had set about designing a horizontal – head literally first – triple with supercharging to replace the V4. But Harry Collier was suspicious of Craig's motives and that he might amount to a Norton spy. So he allowed Craig to work on his racing twin while bringing in Vic Webb and later on Phil Irving – of Vincent fame – to work in secret on the new racer.

Craig was working on military projects, fitting in his dream twin in his spare time. He initially envisaged a parallel twin with supercharging, called project E90S – S for supercharging – which was influenced by the BMWs that had won the final pre-war Senior TT. It is probable that

The Team Obsolete Porcupine paraded on the Isle of Man.

the water-cooled cylinders were vertical, and certainly there was a supercharger and unit-construction gearbox, a rarity in British motorcycles. Projected power was 65bhp, 10bhp more than the much heavier V4. The chassis was designed by Phil Walker, who would later pen the AJS 7R sohc 350cc single. Unfortunately, AMC chairman Donald Heather insisted that all AJS racing models used the firm's own woefully ineffective Teledraulic forks and poor Jampot shocks, which were greatly inferior to the Nortons' Girling suspension. Joe Craig is said to have seen the 2-cylinder engine tested on a dynamometer before he returned to Norton in 1946. Phil Irving had already returned to Vincent, taking AMC's development engineer Matt Wright with him. And then, just as the Colliers felt things couldn't get worse, the FIM banned superchargers on racing motorcycles in September 1946. The new AJS racer was beaten before it had even turned a wheel.

THE PORCUPINE IS CHRISTENED

An urgent redesign dropped the near-square (68 x 68.5mm) cylinders to 15 degrees above horizontal, mimicking Harry Collier's pre-war design for a triple. The widely spaced camboxes were originally intended to offer space for intake ports for the supercharger output and maximize cooling. However, they now masked the barrels but housed the hairpin valvesprings for the redesigned conventional inlet ports. Vic Webb drew up transverse fins broken up into a number of pieces (the 'porcupine quills') to assist airflow and so cooling. The E90 had its famous nickname.

Yet this was far from being the most innovative or unusual part of the engine design. A gear train, similar to that seen on many Italian racing motorcycles, drove the twin camshafts as well as the magneto and oil pump. This took oil to the main and big ends while a second pump supplied jets spraying oil onto cam faces. The 360-degree crank raised and lowered the pistons in unison. Unlike other parallel twins the E90's crankshaft was a machined one-piece forging with straight-cut primary drive gears, forged RR56 aluminium con rods and Vandervell plain insert bearings. But this was a lightweight design intended to be supplemented by the mass of the supercharger, the mounting point for which remained on top of the vertical 4-speed Burman gearbox. The supercharger would also have kept the motor spinning – without it, the Porcupine would be prone to stalling in slow corners.

Other features pointed to the intended supercharger. High combustion chambers had valves set at a 90-degree included angle: Norton would start selling twins with a more efficient, narrower, 58-degree angle within a year or so. Intake flow entered via a long curved inlet from two Amal GP 1¹/₈in (28.5mm) Amal GP carburettors, which were supplied with fuel by a single cylindrical float bowl between them. This might not have been a problem with forced induction, but it instead had to rely on the pistons' suction from a

distance. Ted Frend, a Porcupine racer, would years later say that carburetion had been the bike's greatest problem. But resources were tight, the British economy was struggling to recover from the ravages of war, and AMC had to cut their cloth accordingly.

CRUMPETS FOR CLUTCHES

That the project had been kept secret was proven by the surprise of the journalists invited to the official launch at AJS's Plumstead factory in May 1947. As well as noting the Porcupine nickname, the press also described the beautiful vented clutch as looking like a crumpet. Claimed power was 40bhp at 7,600rpm, probably less than a Manx Norton and the AJS weighed 170kg (374lb) – 20 per cent more than the Manx.

The Porcupine also remained lumbered with the AMC forks that were based on the War Department Matchless 350's items, and the oil and air rear Jampots. Its race debut at the 1947 Senior TT would be testing.

The Team Obsolete bike is owned by Rob Iannucci and ridden by Dave Roper.

Jock West, now also AMC's sales manager, and Les Graham were the factory's team, although in truth AMC had no race department and no real experience of racing. The lack of flywheel effect and drag from the plain bearings made the motorcycles almost impossible to start. Clutch trouble slowed West in the race but at least both Porcupines finished, Graham in ninth, West dead last in fourteenth. But at least they finished – twenty-seven riders had started this first post-war Senior TT. The E90 did win the inaugural post-war BMCRC Hutchinson 100-mile event, Frend riding at an 87.17mph (143.26km/h) average. But otherwise a few highlights could not hide the lack of development and experience at AJS.

After a year of supposed improvement, none of the Porcupines finished in the 1948 Senior TT. Chairman Donald Heather realized that the project needed to be either abandoned – expensive and humiliating – or moved up a gear. He therefore asked Matt Wright (back from Vincent, with Irving planning to return to his native Australia) to oversee a new development programme. Wright set about reducing the included valve angle to 79 degrees, and added a deflector in each port to

encourage turbulence and improve combustion. Power rose to 50bhp, but Heather still required him to use AMC's own rear suspension units and forbade streamlining. Ultimately the AMC race department circumnavigated the ban on alternative rear suspension by rebuilding the Jampots with internals from Rover car dampers. When engine airflow pioneer Harry Weslake offered his services, Heather also turned him down, as (perhaps fortunately for AMC, givne their rivalry with Norton) did Joe Craig at Norton.

1949 was the first year of the new World Championships, with the Senior TT the opening round of the Blue Riband 500cc class. The Duke of Edinburgh started the Senior TT, which saw a tie for the lead at the end of the first lap between the AJS Porcupine of Les Graham and his team-mate Ted Frend. Unbelievably, they were then chased by Bob Foster's Moto Guzzi Bicilindrica, almost identical to the bike Stanley Woods won the 1935 race with.

Frend crashed at Glen Helen on lap 4, allowing Foster to lead the race. Two laps from the finish Foster's challenge ended when his Guzzi's clutch failed at Sulby, which moved Gra-

That famous crumpet clutch and steeply down-drafted carburettors. BONHAMS

ham back into the lead from Norton's Harold Daniell.

Graham's luck looked to be holding as he started the last lap with a 90-second lead, before the news came through that he was pushing the AJS at Hillberry. Jock West ran alongside him shouting encouragement, Graham pushing in the final two miles for 10th place. The magneto drive had failed, a too-regular occurrence due to the rigid gear drive that ran it. Eventually it would be replaced by a more forgiving chain drive.

So Harold Daniell was the winner of the first ever 500cc (now MotoGP) round of a World Championship, with Norton team-mate Johnny Lockett second and Velocette-mounted Ernie Lyons third.

VICTORY AT LAST

Once again, things could only get better – and this time they did. Graham recovered to take victory in Switzerland on Berne's gruelling Bremgarten circuit – the Porcupine's first Grand Prix win – and won again at the penultimate round, the Ulster Grand Prix. Graham had finished second to Nello Pagani's Gilera four at Assen, Holland, and was forced to retire with a split fuel tank at Spa Francorchamps, a race won by team-mate Bill Doran. Only a rider's three best results counted that year, however, so even before the season finale,

the Italian 'Nations' Grand Prix at Monza, Graham had done enough to claim the World Championship. This would be the only time a 2-cylinder motorcycle would win the top flight 500/MotoGP World Championship.

Other teams learned to be smarter much more quickly than AJS. Norton's new Featherbed chassis made the Manx faster, while Joe Craig's full race simulations with a dynamometer made them reliable. And Norton had the remarkable talents of Geoff Duke. Gilera and new boys MV Agusta saw that the Norton's handling made even its limited power more usable. Both the Italian factories quickly copied Rex McCandless's ideas. AJS lacked the resources to keep up, as well as the will in upper management to understand what was needed to win.

There was progress, just not on the scale of Norton and the Italian factories. The Porcupine's 21-inch wheels shrunk to 19 inches, but that was really the only lesson learnt from the Norton Featherbed. Engine oil was moved to a new sump under the engine, into which preheated oil could be poured to aid starting. Wheelbase and weight were reduced, but reliability was not. In 1950 Graham suffered two DNFs (as did Duke, but tyres rather than the motorcycle were the issue) in 1950, although he did manage a single win at the Swiss Grand Prix. Graham finished the season a distant third in the championship behind winner Umberto Masetti and Gilera, with Duke only just beaten into the runner-up spot.

The Team Obsolete 1954 AJS Porcupine on show in the USA. CRAIG HOWELL

Alternative view of the stripped E95. BONHAMS

Frustrated by a lack of development with the AJS, Graham joined MV Agusta for 1951 although he initially struggled to adapt to the very different 2-cylinder machine. AJS made Bill Doran their lead rider, but the year was like the previous season writ large, with Duke the champion and the Gileras pushing AJS into fourth place in the championship.

ALL CHANGE – THE E95

For 1952 the Porcupine was completely overhauled by Ike Hatch and Phil Walker, and the factory designation was changed from E90 to E95. Just four of the new motorcycles were built, the most obvious change being lifting the engine's cylinders up to 45 degrees from horizontal, which allowed a shorter wheelbase. The engine featured a stronger crankshaft, a pressed-up item with one-piece connecting rods and roller big ends replacing the E90's one-piece crankshaft and shell-type bearings. There were improvements to the cylinder head, replacement of the cooling spikes by normal fins being made possible by the improved cooling afforded by raising the cylinders, although the Porcupine nickname stuck. A chain drive was introduced for the magneto, replacing the spur from the camshaft gear drive, aiming for a softer loading that would

bring an end to the constant magneto shaft breakages. Many more parts were in magnesium alloy.

The E90's loop frame was replaced on the E95 with a frame using the engine as a stressed member; the engine was mounted lower, in an attempt to mitigate the higher centre of gravity created by angling the cylinders upward. This also allowed more flexibility in exhaust length and, along with reverse cone megaphones, attempted to broaden the power-band and reduce megaphonitis. The carburettors could now be placed much closer to the inlet tracts and, now angled at 25 degrees, improved fuelling enormously. An alloy scoop below the fuel tank directed cool air towards the bellmouths.

However Matt Wright, who had undertaken the previous redesign, went on record to proclaim 'this whole project was a total waste of effort', although initially the results told a different story. The E95 enjoyed a dream debut, new recruit Jack Brett and Bill Doran finishing first and second, respectively, at the season-opening Swiss Grand Prix, with New Zealand star Rod Coleman in fifth place.

Another new addition to the AJS team for 1952, Coleman had first been given an E90 to try at the 1951 Ulster Grand Prix, following it with a strong showing at the Nations Grand Prix at Monza. In his book, The Colemans, he recalls the speed of the Porcupine:

Dave Roper on the E95 at Gooseneck. IOMTT.COM/ DAVE KNEEN/PACEMAKER PRESS

In the race it was quite definitely faster than the Nortons and I had little problem getting past Geoff [Duke] and Ken [Kavanagh] with just three Gileras only a short distance ahead. I did get with them and found again that the Porcupine was just as fast as the Gileras but was down a little on acceleration from the slower corners, but not by much. I was just beginning to think I had every chance of second place behind Milani when the motor stopped.

Yes, yet another magneto shaft failure.

But the simple results sheet from the 1952 Swiss Grand Prix was far from the whole truth: the works Gilera, MV Agusta and Norton all failed to finish. As the season rolled on the AJS was no match for the speed and reliability of those motorcycles and the factory didn't even bother to attend the final round of the championship at Montjuic Park, outside Barcelona.

Coleman would bring his bike home in the championship fourth place, the highest placing for the Porcupine, matching Doran's placing the previous year. But Coleman's round-by-round results were a fair bit shy of what Doran had managed in 1951 and, in truth, AJS management seemed more interested in playing a blame game rather than moving forward. For 1953 Coleman jumped between his Norton and the factory AJS to finish the year tenth, the only big change to the bike being a reversion to a loop frame. With Reg Armstrong and Geoff Duke taking their knowledge of how Norton had achieved their handling prowess to the Italian factories, they were quickly rising to dominance. AJS's works rider Doran, only competing the first three (of eight) rounds, was a lowly fourteenth in the championship at the end of the year.

For 1954 AJS hired the man then considered to be England's top racing and development engineer at the time, Jack 'CJ' Williams. Father of the famous racer and engineer Peter Williams, he had actually been christened Cecil John Williams. He was presented in public as CJ, because everyone called him Jack and while he was at Vincent they had another rider called Jack Williams. Only Peter Williams' godfather (and racer of note) Jock West regularly called him John.

Jack Williams had been a successful racer before the war and a development rider with Vincent afterwards. He had worked with Matt Wright at Vincent and got on well. Unsurprisingly he replaced the Jampot rear suspension units (as everyone, including Wright, had wanted to) with the Girlings preferred by every other team. New rubber sleeves prevented the problem AJS had with the carburettors shaking themselves loose. A new pannier fuel tank (which lowered the centre of gravity and overall height) needed an alternating current fuel pump which, along with a dam system and header tank, solved the fuelling issues exacerbated by carburettor floats chattering with the engine's vibration. This system required mechanics standing the bike on its rear wheel to prime the internal header tank for starting.

The result of this development was a much smoother engine, which now produced a maximum of 54bhp at 7,800rpm. Bob McIntyre, Derek Farrant and Rod Coleman were the riders, the latter providing the Porcupine with its best international results of 1954. He was placed second in Ulster and won the Swedish Grand Prix, but neither were World Championship rounds that year. Other riders to swing a leg over the Porcupine during its short career included Bill Lomas, Robin Sherry and Reg Armstrong.

UNBEATABLE COMPETITION

Sadly the Porcupine did not go out in a blaze of glory. McIntyre and Coleman both managed a fourth place, at Spa and Assen respectively, their best results of the year. Coleman retired as often as he finished – three times for both – but was still the highest placed AJS in the 500 World Championship: a lowly twelfth with just five points. The E95 might have been an improvement on the E90, but the Italian bikes – MV Agusta, Gilera and Moto Guzzi – could run away from the AJS. By now the Manx Norton was probably as powerful as the Porcupine but was far more lithe and better handling.

And with Norton now also owned by AMC, the Porcupine was very much surplus to requirements. To some eyes that inaugural World Championship looked like a lucky fluke, and perhaps it was. But the E90 and E95 were the final attempts by a British factory to build an original and innovative Grand Prix racer at the cutting edge of what was then possible. That it was achieved on the most frayed of shoestring budgets compared with other factories' resources makes it an astonishing motorcycle. Had the Porcupine succeeded it would now be remembered for its innovation: the unit construction engine and gearbox; primary gear drive; and modern chassis with hydraulic damped telescopic fork and swingarm.

There were really only two reasons for the Porcupine's failure to capitalize on early success. The hasty and incomplete revision of an engine intended to be supercharged that failed to incorporate best practice was the first. This was largely due to AJS management making the classic mistake of starting a project that needed more intensive development – and cash – than they were either willing or able to commit to. The E90 and E95 are glorious reminders of a time marked by experimentation and possibility, rather than by the complacency and lack of development that ultimately killed the British motorcycle industry.

With the death of AMC founder Charlie Collier in 1954, AJS and Norton withdrew from direct involvement in Grand Prix racing at the season's end, never to return. Sadly AJS's development engineer died the same year, leaving a big hole in the racing department. The accountants might have been happy with the withdrawal from racing, never being entirely convinced by the mantra of 'racing on Sunday to sell on Monday'. They were more worried by the rise in popularity of ever-cheaper cars decimating the market for the 'grey porridge', ride to work, motorcycles.

But the record books tell the story: between 1949 and 1954, Porcupines finished twenty-four races with five wins, seven second places and one World Championship. In total,

Rob Iannucci with Dave Roper on the Arter Matchless also run by Team Obsolete at the Classic TT.

only four complete E90 and four E95 machines were built. Only one E90 survives, in the Sammy Miller Museum in England. With the exception of the E95 acquired later by privateer Tom Arter, they were raced exclusively by the works team and never offered for public sale. Fortunately, all four E95s survive today. Two are in a Chartered Museum and one in the Barber Museum in the USA; one other is in private hands, owned by Team Obsolete.

Quoted in *Motorcycle Sport and Leisure* magazine (August 2011) Team Obsolete's Rob Iannucci enthused about the Porcupine:

> *It's the Holy Grail of British motorcycles. It was conceived in the darkest days of World War II, and was created on limited budgets during the austerity of post-war Britain by dedicated men who were passionate about their craft. Yet they created a motorcycle which won the 500cc World Championship, and in my opinion was a truly beautiful mechanical object... it's a two-wheeled work of art.*

Who could disagree?

MATCHLESS G50

As we have seen, a Matchless ridden by one of the founders, Charlie Collier, won the first single-cylinder race at the first Isle of Man TT in 1907. Manufactured in Plumstead, London, between 1899 and 1966, many motorcycles were produced under the Matchless banner, from small 2-strokes to 750cc 4-stroke twins.

AJS was bought up by Matchless in 1931 and Sunbeam was added in 1937. That year the marques were brought under the umbrella of Amalgamated Motor Cycles, which became Associated Motor Cycles (AMC) in 1938. AMC would go on to become the parent company of Norton (in 1952), James and Francis-Barnett. After World War I, Matchless largely fell

out of love with racing, apart from a brief and unhappy flirtation with an ohc 350 single in 1923. In less than a decade they would inherit the AJS 7R and be happy to campaign that motorcycle, building the marque's racing pedigree with the Porcupine post-war. Thoughts did turn to a return to racing around 1950 but, with AMC's acquisition of Norton, it would have been pointless to build a 500 version of the 7R that would be competing against AMC's own Manx M30. In any event, as the Jampot rear suspension episode related in Chapter 5 proved, AMC's management were understandably of the belief that their racing efforts should reflect what they had in the showrooms.

1949 AJS 7R – the model that AJS were selling as an over-the-counter racer, which was the template for the Matchless G50. BONHAMS

ABOVE AND BELOW: **1960 Matchless G50.** BONHAMS

Matchless was one of the last of the big British marques to follow the move from singles to parallel twins as range-toppers. They announced their first effort, the G9, in 1948 a decade after Triumph introduced the Speed Twin. The G9's 498cc engine was unusual in having a third, central, crankshaft main bearing; this helped with the inevitable capacity increases, which culminated at 646cc in autumn 1958 with the launch of the Matchless G12 and the near-identical AJS Model 31.

Although he rode a Triumph in the movie, actor Marlon Brando was famously seen perched on an export Matchless Scrambler G9 in publicity stills for the controversial 1953 film *The Wild One*. So despite evidence, in the form of AMC's Manx and 7R, suggesting that you needed the robust simplicity of an ohc single to be competitive in Grand Prix racing unless you were prepared to build a transverse four, the Matchless race shop was handed the drawings of the G9 twin. It was like the line from *The Wild One* when Brando's character was asked what he was rebelling against. He replied 'What've you got?' Well, a pushrod twin that should be easier and cheaper to run – if heavier and slower – than an ohc single.

The new model was dubbed the G45, the '45' indicating the projected horsepower. This would be less than a Manx M30 (but much more than the G9's 26bhp) in an inevitably heavier motorcycle, despite the engine becoming an all-alloy unit. The chassis was based on the AJS 7R and first appeared at the 1951 Manx Grand Prix with Robin Sherry in the saddle, eventually finishing fourth after a promising debut. In fact the machine was not an entirely new design but essentially a hybrid of AJS 7R cycle parts with a tuned Matchless G9 roadster engine. The engine's bottom end remained more-or-less stock G9, but there was a new aluminium alloy cylinder barrel and head with distinctively finned exhaust rocker boxes. Fuel was supplied by a single Amal TT (reflecting the G9's sole carburettor), and exhaust was via short megaphones.

The entry was controversial because the Manx was supposed to be a purely amateur event. AMC circumvented protests by promising a production version for 1952, with much further tweaking including twin carburettors. In 1952 the prototype G45 gained more valuable publicity and controversy when Derek Farrant – later an AJS works rider on both the Porcupine and 7R3 – won the Senior Manx Grand Prix after leading from start to finish.

Riders loved the speed and handling of the G45 but vibration, oil leaks and breakdowns (even for the factory bikes) were significant downsides. In an amateur event such as the Manx the G45 might have been a useful tool, on the Grand Prix circus it was simply too heavy and not powerful enough.

Despite the factory claiming that up to 54bhp was possible, it was later admitted that this was a one-off snatched dynamometer reading aimed at pacifying furious directors. Given the considerable overlap within AMC, the problems with the G45 make it remarkable that just a few years after its demise in 1957 the Norton Domiracer project surfaced.

ABANDONING THE G45 FOR A G50 DEVELOPED FROM THE AJS 7R

So 1958 was the last year of G45 production and the AMC race shop bit the bullet and designed a 496cc (90 x 76mm) AJS 7R that the world was told to call a Matchless G50. 180 were built between 1959 and 1962. Immediately competitive, it had power comparable to the Manx 30M but at a few hundred fewer rpm. It also weighed 129kg (285lb), a tidy saving on the robust Manx's 142kg (313lb).

While AMC's accountants doubted that taking the Porcupine 'racing on Sunday to sell on Monday' was a shrewd investment, the AJS 7R launched the year after the E90's unveiling might well have been. Introduced in 1948, the 7R was a 348cc sohc single that looked remarkably like an updated Velocette KTT, although that was hardly fair. But, like the KTT, the 7R (quickly nicknamed the 'Boy Racer') was intended to be sold as an over the counter racer that would allow privateers to be competitive in Grand Prix racing, if not fighting for the podium. Nonetheless Geoff Murdoch took his 7R to fourth place in the 1948 Senior TT, only beaten by Manx Nortons with an extra 151cc: in other words 43% more cubic capacity than Murdoch's AJS. It was no fluke either and Les Graham would repeat the trick in 1950.

Built from 1948 to 1963, the AJS 7R was one of the most – quite possibly *the* most – successful off-the-shelf racing 350 motorcycle of all time, until the arrival of the Yamaha 2-strokes around 1970. Although the G50 was a new design by Phil Walker (encouraged by AMC sales manager and racer Jock West) with its chain-driven overhead camshaft, it was very reminiscent of the AJS racing 350 and 500 singles of the pre-war era. That included the AJS R7, a 350cc model that had established a number of world records, including two hours at an average of 99.5mph. Despite the fact that the R7 was not as fast as its main rivals – the Velocette KTT and overhead cam Norton – it was surprisingly popular and survived the move from Wolverhampton to Plumstead when AJS was absorbed into AMC in 1931.

Michael Rutter and Michael Dunlop about to set off on their 500cc bikes. Rutter's is a Seeley-framed G50. IOMTT.COM/DAVE KNEEN/PACEMAKER PRESS

Although the 1948 AJS 7R owed little to its pre-war name-sake beyond inspiration its appeal to buyers was similar. Its robust and comparatively simple construction endeared the model to the privateer responsible for his own maintenance, and for most racers this comfortably offset the slight speed deficit compared with the equivalent Velocette or Norton, just as it had before the war. The chain (rather than shaft) drive to the overhead camshaft was cheaper to produce and much easier to assemble, especially by an owner working in his shed.

The twin-loop frame and Teledraulic front fork were designed from lessons learned racing the Porcupine. While it remained essentially unchanged throughout production, the engine was regularly upgraded. The valve angles narrowed, the crankshaft became stronger and, in 1956, the original long-stroke 74 x 81mm was changed to the squarer 75.5 x 78mm, to allow higher revs. AMC's own gearbox replaced the previous Burman in 1958, while engine development continued almost to the end of production, by which time the 7R was putting out around 41bhp.

So when it arrived in 1959 the Matchless G50 could trace its roots back to at least 1948 but, despite being introduced too late for top-tier Grand Prix laurels, let alone a World Championship title, it achieved some remarkable successes.

Even though its chain-driven sohc was theoretically inferior to the shaft-driven dohc of the Manx (which should allow more radical valve settings and higher rpm), the Matchless proved a worthy competitor. The introduction of the patented Weller tensioner in the mid-1920s (also used in the original 7R) meant that a simple chain could connect a crankshaft and cam-shaft, where previously chain whip over a long run could skip sprocket teeth with disastrous results. AJS, alongside Italian rival Benelli, took advantage of this new design to offer sporting ohc engines that were less technically demanding to build than the shaft-and-bevel designs; an added benefit was that critical moving parts could be encased in tidy, oil-tight chain cases. This brought relatively inexpensive, simple and comparatively leak-free racing machines within reach of many more riders.

Perhaps the biggest change (apart from capacity) to the 7R engine was the G50's different lubrication system, with external cambox feed hose and drain through the timing cover. Consequently the barrels, heads and camboxes were minus the oilways present in the original 7R motor.

At 496cc from a bore and stroke of 90 x 78mm, the G50's motor was actually shorter-stroke than the Manx (86 x 85.62mm) but short of that bike's full 499cc; both made 51bhp

ABOVE: **Michael Rutter (G50 Matchless) leads Joe Phillips (650cc ER6 Kawasaki).** IOMTT.COM/DAVE KNEEN/PACEMAKER PRESS

The Matchless G50 was a response to the disappointment of the G45. BONHAMS

– the Manx at 7,500rpm versus the G50's 7,200, however. The single-cylinder barrel and head were cast in light aluminium alloy with a magnesium alloy camchain cover, and the cam-box was painted a rather brighter gold than magnesium alloy is usually finished in, to protect it from corrosion. This alloy is often described as 'Elektron', although that is a registered trademark for a specific product originally produced under licence from the German company that first developed it.

SUCCESS FROM THE START

The G50 was immediately popular and, while slightly less so-phisticated than the Norton, it was far simpler to maintain by the average club racer and its lightness made it more agile. The reinventor of the AJS 7R as a Matchless was Jack Williams, a man who would endlessly fine-tune it in search of fractions of a horsepower to keep the G50 competitive during its five short years of life. Williams was AMC's legendary develop-ment engineer, whose son Peter would in turn to achieve some of the most remarkable Isle of Man TT performances ever wrought on a single-cylinder racer with the Arter-framed G50. Sadly even he could never turn the G50 into a TT winner, something that would have to wait until Dave Roper's run in the 1984 Historic TT with Team Obsolete.

Only around 180 original G50s were built in AMC's East London Plumstead factory during those five years of produc-tion with just two colour options: bright blue with a tan seat or bright red and black with a black seat. Despite such a lim-ited run the Matchless had remarkable success at all levels of road racing, and in the US allowed Dick Mann to clinch the 1963 AMA Grand National Championship.

The AMA (American Motorcyclist Association, the US equivalent to the ACU) had initially decided that the G50 couldn't race in the US as it wasn't based on a road-legal model. Matchless solved the problem by announcing a limit-ed-production, road-legal 'G50 CSR' by fitting the G50 engine into the G80CS Scrambler frame – CSR was AMC parlance for Competition Sprung Roadster, used from 1958 for off-road racing models with rear suspension. Even so, when sub-sequently used on road-going models many assumed it stood for Coffee Shop Racer. In any event, the G50 CSR became known as the Golden Eagle after the name was used in adver-tising due to the gold finish of the engine casings, protecting the similarly coloured magnesium alloy they were cast from.

At the TT Derek Powell's G50 was kept just off the podi-um in the 1959 Senior, only beaten by John Surtees on the MV Agusta and a brace of Manxes. Mike (later Michelle) Duff would take another fourth for Matchless in the 1963 Senior TT, beaten only by the Italian fours. Usually the Nortons were

This is a 1962 Matchless G50, an evolution of the AJS 7R. BONHAMS

Cameron Donald on the Ripley Land Seeley G50.
IOMTT.COM/DAVE KNEEN/PACE-MAKER PRESS

faster (and had faster riders), but it was still a remarkable achievement. Duff finished the World Championship in sixth place but astoundingly Alan Shepherd and his G50 was runner-up at the end of 1963 to Mike Hailwood and MV Agusta. Given that Hailwood won every race that season bar a DNF at Assen (which John Hartle won on the Gilera four), Shepherd's second place is one of the most astounding placings in motorcycle racing yet is rarely talked about. He even suffered two DNFs to Hailwood's one.

Phil Read and Duff finished the 1964 World Championship in third and fourth places, respectively, riding a mix of Matchlesses and Nortons. Paddy Driver and Fred Stevens repeated those placings in 1965 solely riding G50s, and Jack Findlay took his Matchless to third place the following year. It was John Hartle's turn to take a G50 to third spot in the 1967 World Championship, his new Metisse chassis the first sign that all the Matchless needed to remain a competitive privateer mount was a new frame.

NEW FRAMES GRANT A NEW LEASE OF LIFE

Around 1963 AMC had started selling G50 power units to the Rickman brothers' eponymous motorcycle and frame business. Rickman had started manufacturing motorcycle frames for off-road racing in the late 1950s, hoping to sell on their ideas and techniques to one of the main British factories. But none showed any interest in buying from Rickman, which

instead started building their own complete motorcycles using components from other motorcycle producers. They fell upon the name 'Metisse', amused that the French used the word to mean a mongrel, although it has other, less savoury, connotations. Demonstrating remarkable humour the Rickmans knew that others would say their mix-and-match motorcycles were mongrels, so set about proving that there were good engines and good frames but that only rarely were the two put together.

The success of Rickman's off-road racing machines led to the design of road-racing frames, and their pairing with AMC's 500 single resulted in the 1964 Matchless Rickman Metisse G50. The lightweight nickel-plated frame was claimed in full racing specification (including magnesium alloy yokes) to be 5.5kg (11.5lb) lighter and to carry the motor 25mm (1 inch) lower than the stock bike. The first examples used AMC front forks and brake, the latter fitted with a large cooling disc, although the Rickmans soon developed their own forks. The subsequent addition of Lockheed disc brakes was a first for both road racing and production motorcycles. With a 5-speed Schaffleitner gearbox conversion, a period test at Silverstone achieved a top speed of 129mph (208km/h) although the owner's handbook from Matchless suggests that the G50 was capable of somewhat more than that. The Lockheed press release for the 1966 Earls Court show would claim that the Rickman was capable of 150mph (240km/h).

The Metisse started to garner a number of road-racing victories, John Hartle's third spot in the 1967 World Championship being the most notable. But although Rickman might have been the first to marry limited-production chassis with bought-in

ABOVE: **The G50's barrel
and head was cast in light
aluminium alloy with
a magnesium alloy cam-
chain cover; the
cambox is painted
a rather brighter gold
than magnesium alloy
is usually finished in, to
protect it from corrosion.**
BONHAMS

**The G50 had just two
colour options: bright
blue with a tan seat or
bright red and black with
a black seat.** BONHAMS

production engines in the modern era, the best known is probably Colin Seeley. The rights and tooling for the G50 were purchased by Seeley from the ailing AMC in 1966, and the G50 has remained available in one form or another ever since. Despite Seeley having a notable racing and motorcycle-dealing career behind him, winning multiple British sidecar championships, it is his frames that made him famous. It was he to whom Ducati turned when they started building V-twins, such was his reputation by the late 1960s. It was he who started the trend for a frame tube that went straight from the headstock to the swinging arm, a concept that would ultimately lead to Antonio Cobas inventing the modern beam frame.

After experimentation during the winter, his first prototype frame, built from Reynolds 531 tubing – with, of course, a G50 motor – first appeared in early 1966. It was 4kg (9lb) lighter than the standard Matchless frame, The prototype featured Manx forks with an 8in (203mm) four-leading-shoe brake by engineer Eddie Robinson, which Seeley would also sell separately. A Manx rear swinging arm with the Norton's conical rear hub and brake completed the package. Production frames would have a swinging arm made by Seeley, and customers could specify four-, five- or 6-speed gearboxes. These models are sometimes referred to as Condors.

Derek Minter – aka the 'King of Brands' – tested the prototype at Brands Hatch and proclaimed it 'the best steering solo he'd ever tried' with the front brake better than the Oldani

normally used on his own Manx. Dave Croxford went on to win the British 500 Championship on a Seeley G50 in 1968 and 1969.

Inevitably, Seeley also built 350 versions using the AJS 7R motor. His rider, John Blanchard, finished third the first time he raced the 350 at the Brands Hatch International in 1966 and at that year's Isle of Man TT was placed fourth in the Senior (with the 500 G50) and sixth in the Junior event. At international level he won at Mettet in Belgium on the 500 and also rode in selected Grands Prix. At the TT in 1967 Blanchard lapped at over 100mph on the 500 Seeley, only to suffer a broken primary chain while in third place. In 1968 Blanchard prepared his own Seeleys and the following year he was sponsored by Bill Chuck Motorcycles. In the 1969 North West 200 he won the 500cc race, breaking lap and race records. Even as late as 1971 the Seeley 500 was capable of top-ten placings in the World Championship, with Tommy Robb finishing the year in seventh place.

THE ULTIMATE G50

But the ultimate G50 must be the Arter-framed special developed by Peter Williams and affectionately nicknamed 'Wagon Wheels' after its cast wheels, an innovation that would become ubiquitous in the world of motorcycling, along with

Peter Williams with the Arter Matchless in the 1970 Senior TT. TTRACEPICS.COM

Rob Iannucci with Dave Roper on the ex-Peter Williams' Arter Matchless on the Isle of Man.

the disc brakes carried on the magnesium alloy castings. The 500cc Matchless single-cylinder engine should have been well past its sell-by date when the Mk3 factory update debuted in 1969. Yet clever engineering – that extended beyond the wheels and brakes to the lightweight Grand Prix Metalcraft frame – small frontal area and clever packaging made Wagon Wheels a winner from the off. Williams told *Motorcycle News*:

The Arter Special Mk3 Wagon Wheels demonstrated and helped to prove several design innovations. It was the climax of that type of motorcycle's development and led the way with disc brakes, cast wheels, compact design and some aerodynamics. Its legacy is to be seen on every modern motorcycle.

The international and domestic race successes were unquestionably as numerous as they were extraordinary. In 1970 Williams and Wagon Wheels were second to the MV Agusta of Giacomo Agostini in the Senior TT, then still a GP championship round, repeating the feat the following year. In 1972 Williams won the Hutchinson 100 on the bike, overtaking Agostini on his MV in the process. Ago promptly fell off, presumably unable to cope with being bested by an ancient British single. Yet never once, during the three years of racing, did Williams fall off Wagon Wheels. Perhaps unsurprisingly, the bike now lives in New York in the care of Robert Iannucci's Team Obsolete.

From then the Yamaha 2-stroke twins took over as the privateer weapon of choice, but even so for a design by then almost a quarter of a century old the G50 could hold its head up high. It would only have to wait a few years before it was competitive in racing once again, when the Classic Racing Motorcycle Club (CRMC) was established in 1980 to preserve and use post-war racing and sports machines.

CHAPTER SEVEN

THE ORIGINS OF THE ITALIAN FOURS

The Italian factories once dominated World Championship motorcycle racing, beating all comers for half a century, and inspiring far more than just the well-known MV Agusta fours. The Japanese adopted the layout, first at Honda on the race track and then in the showrooms, ultimately followed by their compatriots. Their market and road racing dominance has meant that inline fours still set the pace on road and track. Rules banning more than 4-cylinders mean that this is likely to remain the case indefinitely, or until a ban on carbon-based fuels comes into force. Where once racing offered real variety and innovation, experimenting with rotary engines, 2-strokes, turbocharging and any number of cylinders from one to eight (only seven was never tried) the rule makers at the FIM have gradually led everyone to a single point in the upper echelons of motorcycle road racing. Yet the dominant 4-cylinder engines can trace their roots back almost a century, to 1923.

Of course there had already been 4-cylinder motorcycles, perhaps the most famous being the USA's Henderson and Belgium's FN. But these ran the row of cylinders along (rather than across) the motorcycle, with one cylinder at the front getting plenty of cooling air, while each one that followed became at ever greater risk of overheating, especially if raced. This layout also made the wheelbase unnecessarily long, and complicated final drive to the rear wheel.

The long wheelbase and weight of such a layout made everyone assume that an inline 4-cylinder engine could never be made competitive for racing, although Moto Guzzi would return to the concept briefly between 1952 and 1954. Big V-twins had gradually become uncompetitive in racing, no match for the easy-to-handle singles. Eventually everyone assumed that a 500cc single was the ultimate racing weapon, especially when there were already so many good single-cylinder designs readily available to use as a template.

Even so, in 1923 Carlo Gianni and Piero Remor, who had met as engineering undergraduates in Rome, thought differently. They are where the history of the transverse four started, when these two young engineers – one a brilliant mathematician, the other an innovative thinker – became convinced that the perfect racing engine might just be a transverse four. Their proposed layout had all four exhausts facing forward towards cooling air to prevent overheating, the most common failing in an engine in those early days being a broken exhaust valve. 4-cylinders rather than the usual one, or two arranged as a longitudinal V, meant a low reciprocating weight of everything from valves to pistons to conrods, which allowed the engine to spin faster. Torque – the turning effort of an engine – is multiplied the faster an engine turns, so higher revolutions should give more power.

Of course, such an entirely new 4-cylinder engine was inevitably going to be more expensive to develop than a motor with just one or 2-cylinders. So Gianni and Remor were lucky to catch the eye of a wealthy backer in Count Luigi Bonmartini, a pioneering civil aviator and amateur car racer. They set to work on their *Quattro* (four), with a bore and stroke of 51 x 60mm giving 490cc. The 1924 prototype was referred to as a GRB (Gianini, Remor, Bonmartini) with a single overhead camshaft driving exposed hairspring valves. Claimed output was 28bhp at 6,000rpm (although some suggest it was a little less) compared to 22bhp for the Moto Guzzi C4V at 500 fewer rpm. A useful edge, but probably not enough against the much lighter and narrower 500 single.

The Gilera Rondine in glorious colour. PHIL AYNSLEY

Rondine in period. IVAR DE GIER/A HERL INC.

Development of the Quattro stepped up a gear when Bon-martini was joined by Count Lancelotti in 1927 to form a new company, OPRA (Officine di Precisione Romane Auto-mobilistiche). The GRB name was dropped and the motor revised with twin camshafts that were part of an overhaul that took power to 31bhp at 6,400rpm. A second prototype motor was built with a central gear train to a single overhead camshaft to allow comparisons.

What eventually appeared from the OPRA project early in 1928 was to be pretty much the blueprint for all the post-war fours, with a gear-driven dohc head, albeit with a water-cooled cylinder head. This was now making up to 34bhp, 20 percent more than the 28bhp of the 4-valve Rudge single that was probably the most powerful example of a single-cylinder rac-ing motorcycle at the time. But this twin -cam version proved less reliable than the single-cam engine.

The motor was fitted to a non-unit 3-speed gearbox with both primary and final drive by chain. Piero Taruffi, who was recruited to test the motorcycle, was then very much an up-and-coming rider, known for his speed aboard a Norton sin-gle that had been timed at up to 100mph (160km/h). When the OPRA reached 106mph (170km/h) on its very first run, Taruffi declared himself impressed.

SAVED BY SUPERCHARGING

But in 1929 Sunbeam's single-cylinder racers triumphed at the French, German, Austrian and Italian Grands Prix. 1930 was Rudge's year at the Isle of Man, and proof that the sin-gle-cylinder British motorcycles were still the bikes to beat in the Blue Riband 500 class. Bonmartini could see the writ-ing on the wall, the power of his 4-cylinder engine its great strength but also bringing twin weaknesses: poor reliability and wayward handling. He set about selling the project, but when no buyer was found he embraced a new technology that was driving the search for power in piston engines, initially in the aviation world that Bonmartini was so famil-iar with. Supercharging uses a mechanically driven pump to force air into an engine's intake side, rather than rely on the suction of the falling piston. Forcing more oxygen into a motor gives more power, and the more cylinders an en-gine has the better this works because there are more inlet strokes. So Bonmartini pressed on, placing ownership of the project into another of his companies CNA (Compagnia Nazionale Aeronautica) and renamed the motorcycle Ron-

dine (swallow). 1933 development brought full water cool-ing and supercharging of the 490cc OPRA four, alongside a much improved chassis. The bore and stroke were revised to 52 x 58mm and the new motor gave 60bhp at 8,500rpm, an astounding figure at the time and double what normally aspirated British singles were able to achieve.

Taruffi's Norton was stripped to allow the Rondine to share as much of its geometry as was feasible. Taruffi and Amilcare Rossetti raced two of these revised fours in the prestigious 1935 Grand Prix of Tripoli. Moto Guzzi was determined to win the race, fielding five riders, including legendary Irish racer Stan-ley Woods. Unfortunately Giorgi Parodi, a co-owner of Moto Guzzi, had left Woods' paperwork back at the factory. The two convinced the local governor, Italo Balbo, to overlook the matter, but Bonmartini lodged a successful protest and Woods failed to start. Although Woods bore no grudge, Balbo certainly did and would be the force that drove the Rondine to Gilera.

So when Balbo moved from Tripoli to become head of the Italian air ministry, he made very sure than Bonmartini's CNA – principally an aviation business – had problems at every turn, and eventually Bonmartini took the hint. In 1934 Bonmartini sold CNA to the aircraft manufacturer Caproni, which had no interest in the Rondine. Without Count Bonmartini's mon-ey there could be no further progress, so Taruffi approached Gilera. Founder and owner Giuseppe Gilera realized that this was a once-in-a-lifetime chance and bought everything associ-ated with the project, convinced it was the basis of a fine rac-ing machine. He also brought Remor back into the fold, and that is where the story of the Gilera Quattro, and ultimately the MV Agusta multis, starts.

CHAPTER EIGHT

GILERA QUATTRO

Piero Taruffi and the six Rodine were swiftly and safely installed at the Gilera factory in Arcore, alongside the construction and technical drawings. Taruffi and the rest of the Rondine team soon discovered that, while Bonmartini was involved in motor sport for the fun of it, Giuseppe Gilera was a hard-nosed businessman who knew that what he had paid for needed to bring glory to his factory. And that the Rondine absolutely must stop breaking down.

The problem had been suspected in the CNA days when the crankshafts would fail after just 300km or so (under 200 miles). The main roller bearings were modest and loosely fitted to minimize friction. Giuseppe Gilera had already warned Taruffi he would cut his losses and shut the racing department if the difficult to rebuild crankshafts couldn't be made to last more than one race. Around this time the Rondine's compression ratio was increased from 6.5:1 to 8:1 – a big jump that

The Gilera team around 1909 or 1910. PIAGGIO

may have been solely for speed record attempts, or a reflection of improved confidence in the big ends. These now had bigger, caged rollers and throughout the motor it's clear that reliability is what was being chased: lightweight alloy gives way to steel, bearings get bigger and everything get stronger. In the end Gilera claimed 60–70bhp, depending on the fuel used and the supercharger pressure. In other words, no more than the CNA Rondine unless there was benzole added to the petrol or the blower was geared up. The unit gearbox had 4-speeds, a large heel and toe change lever and a dry clutch.

Abandoning the previous sheet metal structure, a new frame in tubular steel appeared with classical triangulation and adopting Gilera's patent rear suspension. Pressed steel girder-style forks held a 21-inch wheel at the front with 20-inch at the rear. Single leading shoe drum brakes were fitted. The weight was of the order of 170kg (375lb), considerably heavier than the original OPRA, but a price worth paying if it was rewarded with a reliable motor. The changes were considered significant enough for Gilera to complain if anybody again described the motorcycle as a Rondine: this was emphatically the Gilera Quattro.

Even so, reliability proved elusive. There was no doubting the speed of the Gilera, which would lead races and set lap records only to break down. But increasingly these were niggling faults such as tyre valves and clutch cables. The team was also gaining tactical experience, learning that the rider with the fastest motorcycle has no need to try to establish a huge lead early in a race. For 1939, modest aerodynamic trimmings and realization that the engine was safe to 8,000rpm – in contrast to Taruffi's insistence that riders never strayed above 7,000rpm – was rewarded with a top speed of 145mph (235km/h). Finally Gilera reaped the rewards of their perseverance, and their brilliant rider Dorino Serafini was crowned European Champion. However, on 3 September that year World War II broke out, Mussolini taking Italy into the conflict on 10 June 1940. Progress would have to wait until the flames of war had died down.

The Gilera factory survived the horrors of that conflict, continuing to churn out single-cylinder motorcycles for the government and escaping damage from the Allies. With peace in 1945, Gilera returned to considering their racing pro-

The Gilera factory in 1925. PIAGGIO

gramme, stunned that both the FMI and then the FIM (the national and international arbiters of the sport) had banned supercharging and anything but the most basic fuel. The racing department at Gilera – and more specifically engineer Remor – had to return to the drawing board.

Serendipitously, in 1940 Remor had been working on an air-cooled 250 Quattro, bringing together all the lessons learned with the 500. Looking at ways to keep weight down – by abandoning water cooling, for instance – and shortening the wheelbase with cylinders inclined at a modest 30 degrees despite the intention to supercharge it. So this, rather than the 500, was where Gilera started their quest to win the inaugural World Championship.

Like just about everybody else in the motorcycle industry, Giuseppe Gilera was convinced that victory in the new-for-1949 500cc World Championship would be the ultimate advertising campaign. Unlike most others, however, he did not believe that the winning motorcycle had to have any connection to what was in the showrooms. Like the British, Gilera's top of the range sporting motorcycle was a 4-stroke single, in Gilera's case the ohv Saturno. This had no realistic chance of beating the lighter, lither, more powerful ohc British equivalents, and doubtless Giuseppe Gilera knew this.

A NEW QUATTRO

Remor's plans for the new 500 four were executed by the end of 1946. The engine retained the same bore and stroke dimensions of the previous Quattro (52 x 58mm) for a total displacement of 492.7cc and a jump in the compression ratio to 9:1. Like the 250 design (and more like a car than most motorcycles) the upper crankcase, cylinders and heads were a single casting. Valves were operated, as before, by a central gear drive to twin camshafts and fed by twin 29mm Dell'Orto carburettors (although some say 28mm Webers). Four separate exhaust pipes (initially without megaphones) were used.

The 4-speed gearbox was a surprise on an all-new design since others were already trying five. The wet muti-plate clutch ran in a heavily finned sump, so there was no need for the Rondine's separate oil tank. Power output was probably in the region of 50bhp at 8500rpm, although Remor was notoriously secretive.

The chassis was as expected. The usual twin-loop frame used pressed steel girder forks and Gilera's scissors-style rear suspension with a plunger spring behind the gearbox. Wheels were both 19-inch. With a 24-litre fuel tank (a 28-litre one was also used) and no aerodynamic aids, it is said to have

Bob Stanley, workshop partner to Sammy Miller at his museum, warms up the Gilera 500.

Sammy Miller rides off on his museum's replica Quattro.

Geoff Duke on the Gilera Quattro at the 1955 Senior TT. TTRACEPICS.COM

weighed just 135kg (298lb). That was actually less than a Manx Norton, proof of how robust a 500cc single-cylinder racing motorcycle needs to be if it was not to shake itself apart.

The first run for the Quattro was by Carlo Bandirola on the straight road at Arcore, right in front of the factory. The first real test was on the Bergamo motorway in the spring of 1948, watched by many. Unloading it, the mechanics remarked on the exceptional lightness, and how easily it started.

This was when another name linked forever to MV Agusta joined the 4-cylinder adventure. Arturo Magni, a friend of Giuseppe Gilera's son Ferruccio, had experience in aeronautical – rather than mechanical – engineering. Remor wanted a very special mechanic for his new engine and race team, and one without previous motorcycle experience. It may seem strange, but Remor wanted a very different skills set to his own, or perhaps someone who wouldn't argue with him. Coincidentally, Honda would go on to recruit aeronautical engineers for their racing multis.

The new Gilera was initially raced by Nello Pagani and Carlo Bandirola, joined by Massimo Masserini for testing. But once

again reliability was an issue and some riders felt that Remor was simply cherry picking ideas from others, notably Gianini and Alfa Romeo, without fully understanding them. Lubrication was a constant problem that Remor either could not or would not address. The feud that this led to with Pagani, in particular, quite probably cost Gilera the inaugural 500cc World Championship.

In 1948 Nello Pagani took the Quattro to its first race in Cesena, but he withdrew claiming the machine was 'unrideable' despite Masserini's protestations to the contrary. Remor was livid and banished Pagani to the Saturno single. Masserini led the Dutch TT at Assen, but dropped back and eventually fell when it started to rain. Only the last race of the year, the Grand Prix des Nations at Monza, was won by Masserini, mainly because Norton and AJS did not start there. Gilera's woes grew further when Masserini announced he would end his riding career at this point, returning to the family business. Bandirola simply fell off too often to become a champion and, although it was clear to everyone else that the handling of the machine was below par, Remor apparently refused to improve the machine.

Despite this, or more likely because they were unaware of Remor's demons, the press were convinced that the 1949 inaugural 500cc World Championship would be won by Gilera. Giuseppe Gilera had now taken over the upgrading of the 4-cylinder motor, alongside Taruffi when he was available. Arturo Magni wrote that these '4-cylinders Gileras on paper should be unbeatable, instead they are repeatedly beaten'. The team left Remor to design a road-going 125 and built three new engines to address the crankshaft and lubrication issues. Rather than being one piece, the crankshafts were five-piece pressed-up affairs that Giuseppe Gilera had originally wanted. This now allowed one-piece – rather than the previous two-piece – bearing cages and con-rod big ends. New oilways improved lubrication, especially to the gudgeon pins, in some ways a return to the CNA Rondine design.

THE NEW WORLD CHAMPIONSHIP STARTS

Gilera skipped the opening round of the World Championship on the Isle of Man, mindful of the huge cost of travelling there and that they did not have a rider who knew the course well enough to challenge for points. These were awarded only to the first five finishers, from ten for the winner down to five for fifth place with an additional point on offer for the fastest lap. However, in the 500 and 350cc classes only the best three results counted towards the title.

The next round was on 3 July at Bremgarten for the Swiss Grand Prix. Switzerland was an important market for Gilera so a good showing here was deemed essential. But, predictably, Bandirola crashed and his team-mate, the arguably inexperienced Arciso Artesiani, took a creditable but distant second to Les Graham and the AJS Porcupine.

Retired racer and TT commentator Steve Plater tries the Bob McIntyre 100mph lap replica for size.

Another view of the Kays' replica Gilera Quattro built to celebrate the 60th anniversary of Bob McIntyre setting the first 100mph+ lap of the TT mountain course.

Remor cannot have been surprised when Giuseppe Gilera wadded in and insisted Pagani was given the Quattro the Dutch TT run at Assen just six days later, on a Saturday as was usual. Pagani's win was effortless, his behaviour on the track making it very clear to everyone watching that with the Quattro he easily had the measure of Graham and the AJS.

As an aside, contemporary press reports mention the number of Japanese who crowded around the Gilera Quattro whenever it was in public view at Assen, taking photographs from every conceivable angle. Clearly there were people on the other side of the world who appreciated that this was the future of motorcycling.

The Belgium Grand Prix was next, on the 17 July at Spa Francorchamps, but Pagani's Quattro failed to run properly with what turned out to be a loose valve seat, although he at least managed to come in fifth and so in the points.

The penultimate round of the championship, the Ulster Grand Prix, was just over a month later at Clady. Although the Gilera was fastest through the speed trap, the advantage wasn't great and Les Graham's win and fastest lap made him champion-elect, regardless of how things played out in the final round at Monza. Gilera's dream was over, although there was the hope that some pride could be restored in their home race, the Grand Prix of Nations.

At Monza, in front of a partisan crowd, the three Gileras were soon leading the race with Pagani, Artesiani and Bandirola in line astern. Les Graham hung onto the trio at an impressive pace until, with tragicomedic inevitability, Bandirola fell taking the AJS Porcupine rider with him. Fortunately neither were seriously hurt. Otherwise most of the spectators got what they had waited for: a Gilera one–two. Pagani's 29-point tally was one shy of Graham's, although he had won the 125 championship as a consolation prize.

The Italian press, however, were having none of it. The fastest lap rule were pored over, because in Switzerland the fastest lap had been set by Ted Frend who failed to finish so the point was awarded to Graham. In the end the FIM confirmed that the point was to be awarded for the fastest lap by a finisher and the points standing was correct. Pagani accepted this graciously, realising Graham would otherwise have ridden to a safe fourth place at Monza, keeping well clear of Bandirola.

REMOR AND MAGNI LEAVE FOR MV

But what really angered Giuseppe Gilera was that Gilera had lost the constructor's championship by a single point to AJS. He understandably blamed Remor, unable to understand why he couldn't work with any of the riders. And by now none of the riders wanted to work with Remor, clearly the fly in the ointment. Whether he was pushed or jumped has never been clear, but certainly Count Agusta was desperate for someone who could build him a bike to beat all comers in the Blue Riband class. So Remor left for MV, although he didn't just take fond memories, even if he had any. Arciso Artesiani and chief mechanic Arturo Magni would join him at MV's Gallarate base after blueprints went missing at Gilera. Giuseppe became increasingly cautious about engineering appointments, and paranoid about secrecy.

Fortunately the trusted Piero Taruffi came back to Gilera and Franco Passoni and Sandro Colombo were promoted, having worked under Remor. As we have seen earlier in this chapter, especially with the redesigned crankshaft and lubrication, by this point in the story it is clear that the real engineering talent is with Giuseppe Gilera and Piero Taruffi. Despite his nickname, *Volpe d'Argento* (silver fox), Taruffi was still keen to pursue his career with Ferrari, and would race an Alfa Romeo for him in the inaugural 1950 Formula 1 championship, but agreed to replace the departing Magni as Gilera's team manager in the interim.

The biggest change for 1950 was that the motor was built up with separate heads and a full-width cam cover, and cylinders bolted to the upper crankcase. This made checks and adjustments much easier than with Remor's larger integral castings. The rear suspension returned to Gilera's usual layout rather than Remor's system. The front brake became full-

Michael Dunlop runs the parade lap – he actually managed a 100mph lap from a standing start. IOMTT.COM/DAVE KNEEN/PACEMAKER PRESS

Note the remote float bowls that allow the carburettors to be angled for a downdraft effect.

width, although the forks remained girders despite the British singles demonstrating the superiority of telescopic forks. Carburettor size increased to 30mm and power was up to 52bhp at 9,000rpm. The riders for 1950 would once again be Bandirola and Pagani, plus newcomer Umberto Masetti.

The World Championship points system was rejigged for 1950, the controversial fastest-lap point gone, and points awarded down to sixth place with the best four results now counting. The races were at the same six venues as the previous year but, as usual, Gilera skipped the opening round on the Isle of Man.

Although Masetti and Pagani led a Gilera one-two home at the second round at Spa Francorchamps, Geoff Duke would almost certainly have won if his tyres had not failed him, as we discovered in Chapter 4. This Belgian Grand Prix was also where Remor's Gallarate 'Gilera' first raced, Artesiani taking the new MV Agusta to fifth place. Having chosen to miss the Isle of Man TT, Gilera was far from certain to win the World Championship.

But six days later Masetti won at Assen, and Duke suffered more tyre woes and crashed. The Gilera team's spirts rose again, only to tumble when they arrived at the Swiss Grand Prix. This had been moved to a short (under 4 miles/c.6km)

street course in Geneva and was held amidst frequent showers that played havoc with a rider's feel for grip. The conditions made the Quattro, with minimal flywheel effect, far trickier to ride quickly than the twins and singles. Remarkably Bandirola held Duke at bay to claim third, behind Masetti who could not resist Graham's bid for victory.

Next was the Ulster Grand Prix and the disliked Clady course. Duke won, keeping his flickering title hopes alight although Pagani deliberately allowed Masetti to pass and claim sixth place, the final points position. Next time out Duke won at Monza, with an exhausted Masetti eventually having to accept second place. He was Gilera's World Champion, but Norton had the constructor's championship that was almost as prestigious in those early days. Again the rider's championship had been settled by a single point, and Pagani's selfless action at Clady. But the Gilera Quattros had at last proved reliable as well as fast, and Masetti had ridden well and wisely. Giuseppe Gilera threw his customary end of season party and then the team sat down to examine the lessons of their campaign.

UPGRADES IN READINESS FOR THE 1951 SEASON

Clearly the first of these lessons was that the Rex McCandless Featherbed frame was in a league of its own, and Gilera quickly adopted its innovations. Frame tubes became round rather than oval, telescopic forks were fitted and twin sprung and damped shock absorbers were fitted at the rear. The motor was upgraded to four carburettors, either 25 or 28mm Dell'Ortos depending on whether conditions demanded better drive or outright horsepower, which now peaked at 53bhp at 9,500rpm.

Alfredo Milani was moved on from racing Saturnos to the Quattro to replace Bandirola, departing for Count Agusta's shilling. The first outing would take the Quattros to Montjuic Park for the first time, at the Spanish Grand Prix held over the first weekend in April 1951. This was now part of the World Championship and, with a French Grand Prix also added to the calendar, took the number of rounds to eight. The points system remained the same but now the five best results would decide the championship. Count Agusta would be fielding four riders in the 500 class including Les Graham, so it would be a real chance to see how the Italian 4-cylinder machines compared.

Much like one another, came back the answer. Masetti took the win in Spain, the only Quattro to finish and inheriting the lead from Milani's broken Saturno on lap 17.

Yet another replica
Quattro lurking in the
pits of the Classic TT.

BELOW: **Another view of
the Bob McIntyre replica.**

Alternative view of Bob Stanley warming Sammy Miller's 500.

Next was the Swiss Grand Prix, back at Bremgarten in horrendous rain, which brought little comfort to any of the World Championship hopefuls. Gilera, as before, ignored the Isle of Man TT despite MV Agusta sending Les Graham over for the Senior. But that race was largely a Norton and Geoff Duke benefit, with Graham's MV 500 failing to finish.

Duke was on fire at Spa and Assen although, to much praise in the press, Milani had gelled superbly with the Quattro and managed second place in both races. He won next time out in France, the Albi course amounting to little more than three 2-mile straights that rewarded power and courage. Once the

teams moved on to the Ulster Grand Prix Duke returned to uncatchable form, taking the win and making it mathematically impossible for anyone to beat him to the championship. Once again, however, Gilera had a fine end to the season at Monza with Milani, Masetti and Pagani taking the top three places in that order.

Given the sheer brilliance of Duke it is surprising that Milani's name is not better known as runner-up in the championship with thirty-one points to Duke's thirty-five. He certainly had praise heaped upon him at the time, while Masetti's achievements the previous year were being dismissed as more luck than judgment. Meanwhile Taruffi was doing all he could to persuade Duke to join Gilera.

Over the winter of 1951–52 the Quattro's motor and chassis were barely tweaked, but there was tentative experimentation with streamlining. The coming season would open in Switzerland, an almost unmitigated disaster for Gilera. The Spanish round was now at the far end of the calendar and the French Grand Prix replaced with a German one at Solitude.

Gilera perhaps foolishly kept on ignoring the Isle of Man TT as Les Graham took the MV Agusta to runner-up spot in the 1952 Senior, beaten by under 27 seconds in a nigh-on 3-hour race by Reg Armstrong and Norton. But Assen was a return to form for Masetti, clearly playing with Duke, powering away for an apparently easy win on the last lap. He managed a similar feat at Spa, but couldn't take advantage of a crash that rulede Duke out at Solitude: he was shaken by a crash of his own that detuned him sufficiently to manage just ninth place in the race. In the Ulster Grand Prix his clutch failed and at Monza Graham's MV pushed Masetti into second place, a result repeated in Spain.

But Masetti had done enough, with twenty-eight points to Graham's twenty-five. Again, though, Norton had the constructer's championship and MV was clearly in ascendance. Gilera also needed to improve sales and jealously eyed the British market. Clearly they could not ignore the Isle of Man TT any more.

GEOFF DUKE JOINS GILERA

Taruffi convinced Giuseppe Gilera to take on British riders, bringing Geoff Duke on board for 1953 with Dickie Dale, alongside Irishman Reg Armstrong. The British riders' input helped Passoni improve the Quattro's frame, ready for the opening round of the championship on the Isle of Man on 12 June. Gilera sent eight machines to the Senior TT for Duke, Dale, Armstrong and Milani, but it ended in disappointment. Only Armstrong finished, down on power but still managing third place behind the Nortons and with Duke breaking the lap record before falling at Quarterbridge.

The bike Peter Duke paraded as a tribute to his father.

Still, 1953 was a good season for Gilera. The Italian factory won five of the eight 500cc class races, with Duke victorious at the Dutch, French, Swiss and Italian rounds. By then he was so comfortably ahead in the World Championship that he didn't start at the final round in Spain. So strong was Gilera now that Armstrong and Milani ended the season in second and third places, while the best placed MV Agusta rider was Bandirola, down in eleventh.

Yet Gilera could not rest on its laurels. On the more technical tracks the Nortons were still hard to beat and, with the departure of Remor from MV Agusta, Arturo Magni had also significantly improved that machine. So Passoni tweaked the Gilera by hanging the engine lower in the frame on the advice of Duke, necessitating a longer, shallower sump. The rest of the engine was also overhauled, with a pair of heads sitting above four separate cylinders and stroke increased from 58 to 58.8mm (bore remained at 52mm), raising capacity from 493cc to 499.5cc. But the Quattros' weight was creeping up, mitigated by power output rising to 64bhp at 10,500rpm.

It was soon realized – even before the first 1954 World Championship round at Reims in France on 30 May – that the revisions had created a problem with breaking valves, which would prevent Duke or Armstrong's challenging. New recruit Pierre Monneret saved Gilera's blushes with a popular home win, but it was a daunting start to the season.

Gilera had had to learn about new recruits, as Count Agusta's chequebook had continued to spin an off-season merry-go-round of riders, with Dale the latest to move to MV. Money was clearly becoming an issue, as Gilera would skip the third round of the championship, the Ulster Grand Prix on the 26 June, the event having moved permanently to Dundrod the previous year. Unable to agree suitable terms with the organizers, Giuseppe Gilera refused to attend, although it might have had something to do with the Senior TT held eight days previously.

That race had been delayed by 30 minutes by the torrential rain that the Isle of Man can do so well. Ray Amm and his Norton, however, seemed completely unfazed by the conditions and had a good minute in hand over second-placed Duke. When the race was shortened from six laps to four after Duke had stopped for fuel and Amm had ridden straight on, Giuseppe Gilera smelt a rat and protested to the ACU that the Norton team had been tipped off. The controversy was such that the FIM excluded the results from the World

Another shot of the Sammy Miller museum's Quattro.

Sammy's bike uses a modern electrical tachometer but the originals had no more information to offer the rider.

Championship. The truth is difficult to be sure of: in the conditions Amm had been faster than Duke and the Norton used less fuel, so Amm might have been planning a splash and dash.

In the end it didn't matter, Geoff Duke winning the next five Grand Prix in a row. The last of them, at Monza, was where Taruffi wheeled out a slab-sided prototype dustbin fairing for Duke. This allowed the bike to top 150mph (240km/h) and helped Duke to a comfortable win.

Once again, over winter there was a rider reshuffle as Count Agusta lured Massetti away from Gilera and Amm from Norton to ride for him in 1955. Tragically, Amm was killed in his very first race for MV Agusta at a season-opening race at Imola, falling from the 350 four that MV had introduced in 1953.

1955 would be a difficult year for Duke. The Gilera continued to suffer from valve-train issues that were probably connected to the misfire that first cost him the lead and ul-

timately prevented him from finishing the opening round in Spain. But there was no mistake at the next round in France. Taruffi produced a revised dustbin fairing and Duke lapped all but Liberati and Armstrong on his ride to victory.

The fairings were left off for the Senior TT on the 10 June 1955, but despite this Duke and Armstrong took first and second by some distance. Duke was initially credited with achieving the first 100mph lap of the mountain course, but timekeepers subsequently downgraded it to 99.97mph.

A fortnight later the Circus went to the German Grand Prix, held for the first time on the Nürburgring Nordschleife, a 15-mile (24km) course Duke had not raced on before. Despite a challenge from BMW's super lightweight twins – just 125kg (275lb) – with works rider Walter Zeller joined by none other than John Surtees, by race distance Duke had prevailed.

PUNISHED FOR SUPPORTING PRIVATEERS

Another broken valve at Spa denied Duke a finish, but the podium was still an all-Gilera affair. Six days later, on Saturday 3 July, Duke and Armstrong resumed their usual places on the podium at Assen, having vocally supported a privateers' strike for better start money – this was an act that the FIM would spitefully punish in a manner that would make it impossible for Duke to defend his championship with Gilera. It might not have helped that once again Gilera skipped the next round, the Ulster Grand Prix. More valve-train problems denied Duke a win at the final round at Monza, Masetti taking victory for MV Agusta. But it did not matter, Duke was 500cc World Champion for the fifth time, including a hat trick for Gilera, in the seven years the title had been awarded.

Yet at races at home Duke was effortlessly pursued by his nemesis, John Surtees. Despite approaches from Gilera, Surtees would enter the world stage with MV Agusta in 1956 – fortuitously, given that Gilera would soon be gone from that arena, although nobody suspected it at the time. Duke suffered a further blow as the FIM announced he and Armstrong were banned from the first half of the year for supporting the privateers' strike at Assen. This took on greater significance when it was further announced there would be just six rounds of the championship in 1956, with the Spanish and French rounds gone. Yet the results from four finishes still counted so Duke's season started on 1 July with the Senior and Dutch TTs already decided in Surtees' favour.

Taruffi was now gone entirely to car racing, and Passoni's overwinter revisions had strengthened the Gilera Quattro's chassis and made the dustbin fairing less susceptible to cross-

Sammy Miller runs the 500 Quattro around the car park to the delight of visitors. Note the Spartan fairing.

winds. Megaphones lifted power to 70bhp at 11,000rpm, but these changes had added considerably to the weight, now 150kg (330lb) – 20 per cent more than the original Quattro.

Duke led in his first race of his season at Spa on the 8 July and was timed at almost 160mph (260km/h), but a piston failure cost him a victory that Surtees was only too happy to steal, adding to his points tally accumulated during Duke's ban. The championship looked impossible until Surtees fell at the next round, the German Grand Prix at Solitude, breaking an arm. But Duke was unable to capitalize on Surtees' misfortune with another mechanical failure at Solitude and then a crash in the Ulster Grand Prix, a round Gilera now had to attend if they were to have any hope of retaining Duke's title.

Monza provided some comfort at the end of the season, Duke winning despite Liberati being given a more powerful motor in the hope a popular home win in front of a partisan crowd. Despite that, on that Sunday 9 September 1956, Duke, Liberati and Monneret – in that order – filled the podium places in the 500cc class.

TRAGEDY STRIKES THE GILERA FAMILY

And then, exactly a month later on 9 October 1956, Giuseppe's son Ferruccio died suddenly of a heart attack, aged just twenty-six. Ferruccio had taken over the racing department, with Giuseppe about to hand over the entire company to him. Unsurprisingly the death had a profound effect on the team, and the development of 1957's engines was also inevitably delayed.

So when Duke returned to Arcore from his customary winter overseas, naturally he detected a lack of motivation in the factory. Suggested changes to the 500 were ignored and a fall at Imola in his first race of the season damaged his left shoulder badly enough for Duke to sit out much of the season. Perhaps Duke's mood was a sense that his own glory days were behind him. Certainly team-mates Liberati, who had often claimed he was better than Duke, and feisty Scotsman Bob McIntyre – installed at Duke's suggestion – were to grasp the opportunities at Gilera without hesitation. So, despite Duke's concerns, the history books show that Gilera had a remarkable 1957.

The opening round of the 1957 World Championship was on 19 May at Hockenheim – a track disliked by most riders – for the German Grand Prix. The unspoken team orders were

that Liberati was to be allowed to win where possible but McIntyre was having none of it. He launched himself into the lead, breaking the lap record in the process. But a temporary glitch that cut his engine out allowed Liberati to take a lead that, despite McIntyre's bike recovering and his pursuit of Liberati raising the lap record to over 130mph (210km/h), was to stand. In the end McIntyre ran out of laps before he could pass the Italian.

The Isle of Man TT was however where McIntyre shone. A new team-mate, Australian Bob Brown, was installed to replace Duke and Gilera brought both the 350 and 500 Quattros to the island. Despite McIntyre having never won a TT, he had shown promise.

The 1957 Junior TT was the opening event of the TT's Golden Jubilee, on Monday 3 June, with organizers and fans alike expecting much. They would not be disappointed. The Junior was initially led by McIntyre who broke the class lap record from a standing start, allowing him to romp to a comfortably win. The result augured well for the Senior to be held, as usual, on the Friday.

McIntyre did not disappoint. From a standing start his opening lap of 99.99mph broke Duke's old record. On the flying second lap McIntyre took just 22 minutes and 24.4 seconds to circulate, an average speed of 101.03mph and so posting the first 100mph+ lap of the mountain course. As the news spread the crowd cheered him ever onward, the feat repeated again on lap three with an average of 100.54mph and then on four and six at 101.12 and 100.35mph, respectively. McIntyre eventually won in 3 hours 2 minutes and 57.2 seconds at a race average of 98.99mph (159.27km/h), giving him more than two minutes in hand over second-placed Surtees.

Surtees had his revenge with a win at Assen, but from then on it was Gilera and Liberati's year. He won the final three rounds at Spa, Dundrod and Monza, although was initially disqualified at Spa after commandeering Brown's bike without telling the stewards. He finished the season with 32 points to runner-up McIntyre's 20 as undisputed 500cc class World Champion.

This gave the Gilera Quattro six 500cc World Championships since 1950, with a brace of titles for Umberto Masetti, a hat trick for Geoff Duke and the 1957 title for Libero Liberati. But with Giuseppe's son dead he was done with racing, regardless of his fellow Italian factories' pact to withdraw from the sport to save money (Count Agusta would renege on the deal). There was a brief renaissance when Duke brought the Quattros out of retirement in the 1960s, but in truth this song was sung and the future lay with MV.

CHAPTER NINE

MV AGUSTA QUATTRO

In Count Agusta's hands, the Remor- and Gianni-inspired four would go on to win every 500 World Championship until 1967, when a 4-valve-per-cylinder triple replaced it to fend off the mighty Honda. But even these triples could clearly trace their roots back to the Rondine, and their 4-valve heads were passed on to the final version of the 500cc MV Agusta Quattro for the 1973 season. These were the ultimate expression of Remor and Gianni's original dream, and provided the necessary weaponry for Phil Read's magnificent last stand against the 2-strokes in 1973 and 1974. Under today's point system Read would have bagged the 1975 title as well, proof that the basic premise of a transverse four first laid out over fifty years earlier would be hard to beat. But MV Agusta's part in this story started quarter of a century earlier, and its origins went back further still.

Founder Count Giovanni Agusta designed his first aircraft in 1907 but, unable to fund development, switched to offering maintenance and repairs for others at his factory in Cascine Costa near Milan. Complete aircraft followed and by World War II the eldest of Giovanni's sons, Domenico, had inherited his late father's title and, together with brother Vincenzo, had taken over the management of the company and was building and maintaining military aircraft for the *Regia Aeronautica*, the Italian air force.

Famously and understandably, at the end of the war, the victorious Allies refused to allow the defeated nations to continue making anything that might be turned into a weapon. So MV Agusta, like Aermacchi and others, had to cease aircraft production and turn to something else: in both these cases motorcycles.

Actually a cambox from a later road-going 750 but – apart from the badged end covers – almost exactly the same as on the racers.
RUSS MURRAY

John Surtees at Signpost in the 1958 Senior TT. TTRACEPICS.COM

But this didn't last for long. The Paris Peace Conference was held from late July to mid October 1946, agreeing treaties that allowed Italy, especially, to resume as a sovereign state in international affairs and to join the United Nations. Germany was more strictly managed but still rebuilt in a way that, hopefully, would maintain peace in Europe. The Agusta family quickly resumed their aviation business, initially with fixed-wing aircraft in 1947 and then, from 1952, building Bell helicopters under licence. As well as a huge income stream, it also gave MV Agusta access to technology their competitors could only dream of.

Some might have dropped the motorcycle business altogether, but Count Agusta had developed a taste for watching his motorcycles win races, and kept a villa in Monza Park for that very purpose. But if he was to carry on supporting winners he would need proven motorcycle engineers as well as the permanently open chequebook that he would become

famous for. Between 1949 and 1950 Count Agusta poached first Piero Remor and then, at Remor's request, Arturo Magni from Gilera. He set them to work not just on his existing 125 and 250 racers but also to replicate and improve on the Gilera four.

Almost immediately, in April 1950, MV showed a 500 4-cylinder racing motorcycle that was little more than a Gilera clone. Yet it was upgraded in ways that would prove to be ill-advised, such as shaft final drive and torsion bar rear suspension. There were just two 27mm SSI Dell'Orto carburettors and the exhaust system ran four pipes into two. The main difference from the Gilera motor was a longitudinal gearbox to facilitate the shaft drive, which necessitated an unusual gear shift with a lever on either side, one for up and the other for down.

The new engine used a one-piece casting as Remor had preferred at Gilera, but it differed with central spark plugs

John Surtees parades his MV Agusta 500 Quattro at the Goodwood Revival in 2010.

and was square at 54 x 54mm, to give 494.4cc and 50bhp at 9,000rpm.

The gap between the exotica MV Agusta raced and what they sold to the public was even greater than at Gilera. An ohv 250 was the biggest motorcycle on offer until the 600 four was shown at the end of 1966, and MVs never sold in the numbers that Moto Guzzi's and Gilera's road bikes did. But it didn't matter to Count Agusta. Helicopters bankrolled his racing, which he loved – as long as he was winning. The Count was infamous for his low moods and high expectations.

For the 1950 500cc World Championship MV entered their copycat Gilera with rider Arciso Artesiani, who had finished third the previous year with Gilera. The pairing's first race, round five (of six) actually claimed points at Spa Francorchamps with a fifth place finish. For the final round at the Grand Prix of Nations, held at Monza, two other riders were drafted in. Irishman Reg Armstrong was offered an upgrade from his Velocette single, and Guido Leoni was also brought into the team. Armstrong did not finish and almost uniquely would move from MV to Gilera: every other rider who raced for both marques would move the other way. Leoni could only manage twelfth, so was out of the points. However Artesiani came third, behind new champion Umberto Massetti on a Gilera and race winner Geoff Duke on a Norton.

For 1951 Carlo Bandirola joined Artesiani on MV's 500s,

the pair finishing the year twelfth and fourteeth in the championship, respectively. At the end of the year Remor left MV, apparently voluntarily, eventually pursuing a career in consultancy after a brief spell at Motom. During 1950 Count Domenico Agusta would also approach Les Graham to ride for him and, frustrated by a lack of progress at AJS, Graham joined the MV Agusta to ride and develop their new 500.

Agusta had always insisted on doing everything his own way, but, almost uniquely, he would be led by Graham. In due course Graham used his engineering expertise, riding talent and diplomacy to convince the Count of a better way forward. Eventually he would oust the shaft drive and torsion-bar suspension, add hydraulic rear shocks and British-made Earles forks and, with Magni, introduce a smaller-bore engine to cure piston failures.

MV's renowned engineer Arturo Magni, who later guided MV riders John Surtees, Gary Hocking, Mike Hailwood, Giacomo Agostini and Phil Read to world title glory, always insisted that Graham was the greatest of them all. But Graham had a stinker of a season in 1951, failing to finish a single round despite starting in seven of the eight available. He had started the season with telescopic forks finally replacing the girders and ran a four-into-four exhaust system at the Isle of Man TT at least. Four carburettors were tried at the final round at Monza and gave more power but less flexibility.

ALL CHANGE WITH REMOR GONE

Despite Graham's poor results with Remor gone, and with Count Agusta's trust established over the winter of 1951–2, Graham and Magni decided they needed to start afresh on the engine. The first big change was to swing the gearbox through 90 degrees so that chain drive and a conventional shift lever could be fitted, the pair taking the opportunity to add a fifth speed to the box. Bore and stroke went from square to 53 x 56.4mm, mimicking MV's 125 racer's dimensions and hoping to improve cooling and reliability. Power was 58bhp at 10,500rpm with four carburettors, although two were commonly used. The four-into-two exhaust system also made a return.

For the chassis Graham engaged another Englishman, Ernie Earles. His own Earles forks had a very small wheelbase change under braking or under compression, unlike telescopic forks, and were much stronger. The disadvantages were weight and the disconcerting way the front end rises when braking, so Graham would choose between them or the telescopic forks on a round-by-round basis. The rest of the frame was also redesigned and, like the British riders at Gilera, Graham chose to switch to British Avon tyres rather than the Italian Pirellis.

1952 was the year the tide turned for MV. The season opener, the Swiss Grand Prix at Bremgarten on 18 May, showed how much the MV had been improved. Graham was second and Bandirola third until a tyre problem forced Graham out, although Bandirola's podium position held. The omens for the Isle of Man Senior TT, less than three weeks away, were good. Graham still wasn't entirely happy with the handling, however and elected to use the Earles forks on the mountain course.

Even so, Duke was the clear favourite to make it five wins in a row in the Senior, especially after leading aboard the factory Norton for four laps. Dramatically, he then pulled into the pits and calmly got off his Norton to retire with severe clutch trouble, leaving the others to fight it out over the remaining three laps.

At the 2010 Goodwood Revival the author was fortunate to be the next person to shake John Surtees' hand.

His team-mate Reg Armstrong was determined to uphold British honour and slowly but surely pulled away from Graham on the MV, his luck holding when the primary chain broke on the Norton as he crossed the finishing line. Graham felt he should have won, his pit stop taking far too long and worrying over an oil leak. A missed gear change was his fault however, and lost him almost the final 1,000rpm where the motor made its best power.

With no points taken in the next two rounds (Assen and Spa) the German Grand Prix at Solitude was critical for Graham and MV Agusta. A close-fought race gave Graham the fastest lap but only fourth place. Another fastest lap next time out at Clady for the Ulster Grand Prix was scant consolation when, again, a tyre issue forced him to retire while in the lead. At the final two rounds – Monza and Montjuic Park – Graham excelled, winning both but losing the championship by three points. If the normally ruthless Count Agusta had insisted Masetti did not start or at least finished no higher than third MV Agusta would have had their first 500cc championship with Graham. Instead Massetti's second place denied that chance.

Even so, Count Agusta had high hopes for 1953. The bike was barely updated, such was MV's confidence, with Cecil Sandford (who had won MV their first World Championship, in the 125 class in 1952) joining Graham in the 500 races for 1953. At the Count's invitation, Graham and his family had moved from England to a house near Verghera. The opening round was the Isle of Man TT in mid-June, a magnificent curtain-raiser for MV when Graham won the 125 Ultra Lightweight TT and eight of the ten finishers were aboard MV Agustas.

DISASTER STRIKES

Tragically that win would prove to be Graham's sole victory on the Isle of Man. Just a few days later, early on lap two of the Senior, Graham crashed heavily as he powered out of the dip at the bottom of Bray Hill. Some say the Earles forks failed, others that he was trying to avoid slower riders. One of the first on the scene was Australia Ken Kavanagh, bringing his Norton to a halt but realizing immediately that Graham was beyond help. Count Agusta was so devastated that he threw his resources into making sure the reasons for the crash were understood and addressed. Naturally he withdrew his riders from the championship, only to return for Monza.

At another level, 1953 proved disastrous for MV Agusta with the incomparable Geoff Duke joining Gilera. He sorted the big four's wayward handling almost overnight, leading a clean sweep of the top three championship places for Gilera, helped by MV's temporary absence.

Bill Lomas was approached to take Graham's berth but had misgivings. He had sampled the 500 the previous year at the Ulster Grand Prix and been so nonplussed that he insisted on racing the sole telescopic-fork version that had only been brought in case spares were needed. Even so he felt the bike was too big, too heavy and handled poorly. Graham's performances had made the team complacent, not appreciating the results were a measure of the man, not the machine.

So Lomas signed for the Count on condition that the bike was heavily revised under his guidance, and that the included valve angle be narrowed in the search for power and a compact cylinder head. But the Count also poached Dickie Dale from Gilera for the 1954 season, who promptly won the team's first race of the year at Floreffe in Belgium with Earles forks and an odd half-fairing that Lomas felt made the already insensitive steering even lighter. At least the bike now had a 6-speed gearbox and new rear shock absorbers built in-house rather than bought in from British suppliers. The Earles forks were tweaked and a variety of fairings tried, but rarely liked, by riders as they exacerbated the handling insecurities of a bike that was already too tall and too heavy.

The team skipped the opening Grand Prix in France, starting the season on the Isle of Man. They arrived with a variety of frames (all with Earles forks) as well as the new 350 that Les Graham had run in the previous year's Junior TT until it failed on the second lap. Essentially a sleeved and destroked 500, it was unlikely to be competitive. Although its 42bhp at 11,000rpm was impressive next to the British motorcycles, it was also over 10kg (22lb) heavier than the singles and far less tractable. Lomas felt his seventh place in the Junior TT was as good as the bike was capable of, running with a dolphin fairing. Dale finished twenty-fifth, the MVs drowning in a sea of singles.

In the Senior TT Dale again opted to race with a dolphin fairing, but Lomas decided upon a simple fly screen. As we have seen, the race was run in dreadful weather and Duke said for years afterwards that it should never have started. Ultimately the FIM was so unimpressed that the results were excluded from the World Championship standings. The delays, and the race being shortened to four laps, handed Norton the win despite protests from Gilera. Dale's seventh place seemed fair, beaten by the Gileras and Nortons. The reasons for Lomas retiring on lap 4 are unclear, but may be connected to his growing frustration that would come to a head at Assen, the next World Championship round for MV Agusta as they skipped the Ulster Grand Prix.

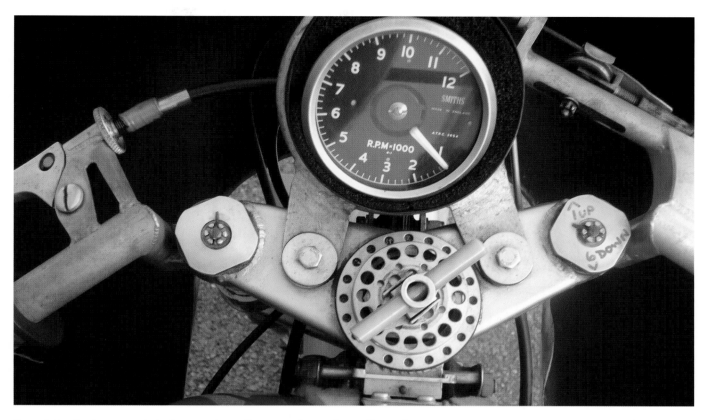

Even John Surtees needs to be sure how the gear change is configured.

LOMAS AND THE COUNT FALL OUT

After another poor showing for Lomas in Assen's 350 race, he started berating Count Agusta through a chain-link fence, loudly complaining about the lack of progress in general and the loathed Earles forks in particular. The count started kicking the wire fence in an attempt to berate Lomas who, in turn, made it clear he would not race for MV Agusta again. That the blame lay with the bikes and not Lomas would be vindicated by his dominant performances for Moto Guzzi over the next few years, becoming the 350 World Champion in 1955 and 1956. As the Italians say, revenge is a dish best served cold.

On paper, Dickie Dale's fourth place in the 1954 500 World Championship gave some comfort; in practice it was solely down to victory in the final round at a Spanish Grand Prix that hardly anyone else outside Spain travelled to. This was because all the World Championships were already decided and all the other factories felt there was no worth in entering. Dig deeper and MV Agusta's fours had a dreadful 1954 and

were clearly a work in progress. Little wonder that Dale left the factory and joined Lomas at Moto Guzzi.

In a move that would be reversed when MV Agusta's main rivals in the 500 class withdrew, Magni and the team went looking for more power rather than trying to make their bike handle as well as the Gilera. In the search for reliability bore and stroke were changed, via cooler pistons, to 52 x 58mm (from 53 x 56.4mm) while revs were increased to raise power to 65bhp at 11,000rpm, swopping piston issues for valve float.

The chassis received much-needed attention, made lower and with the option of MV's own leading-axle telescopic forks at the front and British Girling shock absorbers at the rear. Ray Amm was brought in to replace Dickie Dale, Norton offering Dale little support and choosing John Surtees above him. Dale's first outing was a season opening race at Imola on 11 April, where Amm switched between his own Norton and the 350 four in an attempt to find a cure for the MV's troublesome handling. Unaware of Imola's abrasive surface – the Gileras could barely manage race distance on new tyres – he tried his own partly worn tyres on the MV 350. He fell at Ri-

26 June 1960, Surtees and the MV at the Dutch TT at Assen. NETHERLANDS NATIONAL ARCHIVE

vazza, on the two 90-degree turns just before the run to the start/finish line, chasing Ken Kavanagh on a Moto Guzzi single. Hitting a fence post, he was killed instantly, his tyres' tread completely worn away.

Team-mate Masetti had been lured from Gilera in 1954, despite Gilera occasionally allowing him the race the Quattro. The money was good and friends from his early Gilera years – Magni, Bandirola and Pagani – were already there. Although he was never convinced the MV 500 was as bad as some said, he soon discovered it was not as good as the Gilera. As everyone else at MV Agusta bar the Count seemed to know, the Quattro was too big, too tall and too difficult to get the best from.

As we have already seen, 1955 was the year when everything clicked at Gilera and Geoff Duke was on imperious form. MV didn't even bother travelling to the Isle of Man, in what was ironically remembered as the first year that British machines failed to win a single TT. However, as ever, the final round at Monza was what really mattered to Count Domenico. With Duke out of the race Masetti rode like a madman, pipping Armstrong for the win at the post.

The Count was still looking for a Les Graham replacement when the British MV importer recommended John Surtees, then still just twenty-one. Norton had warned him that they would not be offering support for 1956 but, like many other British riders, Surtees was wary of the MV Quattro's handling and mindful of the deaths of Les Graham and Ray Amm. So he travelled to Gallarate late in 1955 for a meeting with the Count, eventually agreeing to sign if he could ride the 500 and found it to his liking – or at least having the potential to be developed to his liking. This was arranged for February 1956 and must have been satisfactory as Surtees agreed to sign.

The first round of the World Championship was once again on the Isle of Man TT, the MVs tweaked in accordance with Surtees' suggestions. The 6-speed motor was much as the previous year with just an increase in compression ratio, back to 11:1, now that reliability seemed sorted, giving 67bhp at 10,500rpm with strict instructions not to exceed 11,000rpm. The 500 retained siamesed exhausts, with a single pipe on each side, while the 350 had a four-into-four system. The 500 weighed an acceptable 165kg (364lb) but the 48bhp 350

The remarkable MV six that in the end wasn't needed. KLAUS NAHR

weighed just 8kg (18lb) less, compared with the 120kg (265lb) of the Moto Guzzi flat single. Suspension travel was reduced, Surtees certain that it would improve high-speed stability. The front brake now had an air scoop but it was still an SLS. Both the 350 and 500 fours had a half-fairing.

It should be remembered that neither Surtees nor an MV four had ever won a TT, so speculation was rife as to who might win the two big races of the week, the Junior and the Senior, which opened and closed proceedings. Surtees had used the late start to the season to familiarize himself with the big MV by racing it at Crystal Palace and Silverstone. His pair of wins at both events with a 1955 bike bode well for the TT where he would race the 1956 version.

The Junior TT proved to be a three-way battle between Surtees on the MV four, and Moto Guzzi mounted Bill Lomas and Ken Kavanagh. Lomas led for the opening five laps of the scheduled seven, but then retired with mechanical problems at the Guthrie Memorial. Surtees led by less than one second from Kavanagh, but then dropped out at the Stonebreaker's Hut on the last lap, out of fuel with barely 8 miles to go.

SURTEES WINS AFTER CRASHING INTO A COW

In the event Surtees had to revert to the 1955 500 – intended only as his reserve bike – after the 1956 bike was extensively damaged when he hit a cow in practice. Fortunately Surtees was still in a condition to race. His MV, Lomas's Moto Guzzi V8 and Walter Zeller's BMW flat twin were the only entries in the Senior with more than one cylinder. If Surtees had been hurt in the crash his performance did not so much as hint at it. He set the fastest lap of the race and took a comfortable win, coming home over a minute-and-a-half ahead of second-placed John Hartle and his Norton.

The next round at Assen was also – from a spectators' point of view at least – an easy win for Surtees in the 500 class and a creditable second to Lomas on the Moto Guzzi single in the 350 race. But Surtees was still unhappy with MV's chassis, and more than a little disappointed that there had been none of the improvements he'd requested. Like Bill Lomas before him he discovered the Count often seemed uninterested in im-

John Surtees' 500 again at Goodwood.

proving the Quattros but, unlike Lomas, Surtees took a 'softly softly' approach. He booked himself onto the same overnight train the Count was taking back to Italy, where Domenico would have little choice but to listen.

Less than a week later, on 8 July, was the Belgian Grand Prix at Spa-Francorchamps where Geoff Duke was allowed to return to the fray following his FIM ban. A win in the 350 race for Surtees was a morale booster and Duke's retirement while leading the 500 race allowed Surtees to keep in unblemished record of wins in every 500 championship race of 1956. It also made it mathematically impossible for him to be caught in the championship, which was just as well. At the next round, the German Grand Prix at Solitude, he crashed in the 350 race and broke his arm badly enough to end his

season. 1956 had been Surtees and MV Agusta's year, but the following season was to be very different.

While Surtees managed second place in the Golden Jubilee Senior TT, he was two minutes behind Bob McIntyre's magnificent finish in a race in which he had smashed the 100mph barrier in style. Fourth was all Surtees could achieve in the Junior. He won next time out at Assen, due more to others retiring than to the MV getting better. And, apart from a fourth at Monza's season finale, he retired at the three other rounds, only able to offer a third place in the championship to the Count.

In truth, back in Italy the engineers had been focussing on 1958. Moto Guzzi's V8 had become reliable although the handling still needed attention. But it was far lighter than the

This is a works motor. Compare it to the road bike in the next image.

Gilera and MV fours, as well as more powerful. Once Moto Guzzi sorted its wandering ways it would most likely become unbeatable. So the Count was diverting efforts into a new 500cc six ready for 1958, when he was handed an open goal by his strongest competitors.

Count Agusta had been either lucky or shrewd enough to focus on international races, rather than the Gran Fondo races such as the Moto Giro. In 1957, when Gran Fondos were banned and other Italian manufacturers withdrew from Grand Prix racing, the field was pretty much left open to MV Agusta. The dominant marques – Gilera, FB Mondial, Moto Guzzi and MV Agusta – had made a pact to abandon the financially ruinous World Championship, but MV renegaded on the agreement. After all, the Count wasn't in racing to sell motorcycles, but rather to divert profits from the helicopter business into winning races.

With no real competition the Count did not risk racing the six, and it would face competition just once. It was run at Monza in 1958 by John Hartle who complained that it had too narrow a power band for just five gears. MV would revisit the concept when Honda and Mike Hailwood threated their hegemony, testing a 350cc six and being ready to build a 500cc version, but when Honda walked away from racing at the end of 1967, they were again abandoned.

RELIABILITY MORE IMPORTANT THAN POWER

So instead, over the winter of 1957–58 MV returned to the four, looking for reliability given that they knew they would have far more power than the competition. Ironically, with dustbin fairings now banned this was especially advantageous – the Moto Guzzi singles especially used streamlining to make up for a lack of power. Of the seven rounds of the 1958 World Championship Surtees won all but one, usually followed home by new team-mate John Hartle. They didn't even bother travelling up to the land of the midnight sun for the Swedish Grand Prix held at Hedemora. Surtees finished the year with 32 points, Hartle's runner-up spot achieved with 20. Geoff Duke's third place, usually running his own Norton but occasionally a BMW flat twin, came with 13 points. The gap did not reflect Duke's talent, but rather the MV's speed and new-found reliability.

The 1958 TT was marked by MV's total domination of all four solo classes, a classic Junior and Senior double by John Surtees and the first appearance in the TT of Mike Hailwood. Surtees' victorious MV finished almost six minutes ahead of runner up Bob Anderson's Norton in a scene that was to be repeated for many years to come.

The road bikes' motors were remarkably similar to the racers'. Internally the hand-built nature means that parts are not as readily interchangeable as might be expected. This one has a Magni chain-drive conversion, making it closer still to the racers. RUSS MURRAY

Not only was Surtees a brilliant rider, he was also a gifted engineer. Despite MV knowing they would be expected to steamroller the 500 class, Surtees set to work designing a new frame. With wheels now both 18 inches, Surtees developed a hanging-in style that allowed him to retain corner speed while leaning the bike over less, important that now the wide crankcases were nearer the ground.

Surtees won every 350 and 500 championship race in 1959, usually followed home by new team-mate Remo Venturi. Hartle was charged with riding the 350, having been originally recruited to race the dominant 250 twin but promoted when Dale and Lomas left. Hartle duly delivered second place in the 350 championship, far behind Surtees' perfect points tally. Hartle was allowed a 500 for the Senior TT but failed to finish. Surtees' double at the TT made him the only person other than Stanley Woods to win both races in the same week twice. Mechanical problems prevented him from repeating the performance the following year, but he would manage his third double in 1960 on his way to another brace of World Championships. He had won both the 350 and 500 classes three years on the trot and, thanks to efforts of others in the

125 and 250 classes, MV had won all four solo titles in each of those three years. From here onward, however, Surtees decided his future lay with cars, and would achieve the unique accolade of being a World Champion in that world as well.

HONDA AND HAILWOOD ENTER THE FRAY

In the meantime, Honda and rider Jim Redman were making waves in the 250 class. The 250cc RC161 that he inherited from Tom Phillis was an all-new bike, almost a Gilera Quattro in miniature. Remember the Japanese photographers at Assen in 1949 obsessing over the Gilera? This must have been the fruits of their labours. And Honda famously never rested on their laurels, discarding their racers at the end of each season and starting afresh. The 1961 RC166 took the first five places in the 250 World Championship, led by new recruit Mike Hailwood. While he would join MV the following year and take the 500 World Championship,

**Compare the frame and
layout to the road bike.**

Honda was dominating the other classes with 250 and 350 champion Redman.

The Count initially abandoned the 1961 World Championships, with the claim that MV was to focus on domestic racing. But he realized that his lateness in this decision left his proposed lead rider, Rhodesian Gary Hocking, without a ride and did the honourable thing: he agreed to supply Hocking with bikes on the condition that they carried a 'Privat' logo rather than MV branding and that Hocking must accept there would be little or no development.

Although Hocking won seven of the eleven 500cc rounds (with few attending the new season finale in Argentina) the

TT was proof of how special two other riders were. In 1961 MV failed to win a TT, to the delight of British fans. Norton won two, Honda achieved a double and Mike Hailwood became the first rider in the history of the TT to win three races in one week.

Hocking was odds-on favourite to win the Junior and immediately seized the initiative from the AJS of Hailwood, who was dicing with debutant and 1960 Junior Manx Grand Prix winner Phil Read. Hocking was flying and established a new Junior TT lap record of 99.80mph (160.58km/h) on his second lap as he increased his advantage to over a minute. Then he began to slow with engine problems and, after a lengthy pit

ABOVE: **Mike Hailwood and his crash-damaged MV after his fall at Sarah's cottage in the 1965 Senior TT. He still won the race.** TTRACEPICS.COM

An MV 750 upgraded by Arturo Magni is as close as you can get to the experience of the works racers – and even then you'll need deep pockets.
RUSS MURRAY

stop, lost the lead to Hailwood. Read was on brilliant form and pushed the ailing Hocking back to third. Just 14 miles from the finish the gudgeon pin on Hailwood's AJS broke and he ground to a halt, leaving the road clear for Read's remarkable debut victory. Hocking held on to second place.

Hailwood made up for this setback with a truly memorable ride in the six-lap Senior. Again Hocking stormed away on the MV and, by the end of the third lap, comfortably led Hailwood's Manx Norton. But another lengthy pit stop came for the MV, trying to sort out a sticking throttle, dropping Hocking to fifth place. He was forced to retire at the end of the fifth lap when the throttle stuck wide open and Hailwood went on to win. His race average of 100.60mph (161.87km/h was the first at over the ton on a single-cylinder machine.

Unknown to Hocking, the British MV importer was trying to persuade the Count to return to the world stage with Hailwood as his number one rider. To Hocking's chagrin Hailwood was offered a second 'Privat' bike for the final round at Monza, which he won at record speed; Hocking crashed out when he ran out of ground clearance. Hailwood was offered the chance to campaign the 'Privat' bikes in the 350 and 500 classes for 1962.

The first round of the 1962 350 and 500 World Championship was once again the TT in June. Hailwood and Hocking were the sole MV competitors, Honda refusing to supply Mike with bikes in the smaller classes. In the 250 race he rode a single-cylinder Benelli, and in the 125 an EMC 2-stroke. A two-lap 50cc race was also introduced, in which Beryl Swain became the first female rider in a solo TT, and possibly the first woman to race in a World Championship round.

An epic battle waged between Hailwood and Hocking in both the Senior and Junior. The six-lap Junior had Hailwood and Hocking at their very best as they fought a titanic battle round the Mountain Course, although there was also tragedy. Hocking established a 100mph lap from the Junior's standing start to lead his team-mate by 11 seconds. Honda-mounted Tom Phillis was third, but on the second lap he was killed when he crashed at Laurel Bank. Hocking continued at the front, with Hailwood setting a new lap record as he closed the gap.

At half distance the two MVs screamed in for their fuel stops side-by-side. On the penultimate lap Hailwood pulled back a precious second and the stage was set for a nerve-wracking last lap. Despite minor mechanical problems Hocking still held the advantage at Ramsey as they began their final desperate climb over the Mountain. At Keppel Gate Hailwood had pulled the gap back to five seconds and, with a final flourish down the Mountain, he moved ahead to win by the same margin after one of the greatest-ever TT duels.

Hocking led by just 1.6 seconds after one lap of the scorching Senior, but, as the Rhodesian smashed the lap record, Hailwood was in trouble. First he lost bottom gear and then he was in the pits for 13 minutes to have his clutch repaired. He returned to finish twelfth.

But from then on until the end of 1965 Hailwood would win all but two of the 500 races he entered. After his friend Tom Phillis was killed, Hocking abandoned motorcycles to race cars back at home, a decision that sadly ended with a fatal crash.

AGOSTINI ARRIVES

Italian Giacomo Agostini was recruited in 1964 from Moto Morini as development rider for the new MV 350 triple but, in addition, for the 1965 season he would partner Hailwood.

The 1965 season opener was at Daytona, only the second time there had been a US Grand Prix, even if it would be 2007 before another was held. MV sent just Hailwood (there was no 350 race), who not only won the race but set a new record for distance covered in one hour: 144.8 miles (233km). Once again Hailwood dominated the season, winning all but two rounds, ominously losing the late season Finnish Grand Prix to Agostini as he started to realize he had a nemesis.

There had been notice of this at the Isle of Man TT, although Agostini's first Senior TT ended in disaster. In poor conditions, with rain falling on parts of the course, Hailwood led the young pretender by 25 seconds at the end of the first lap. The damp asphalt caught Agostini out at Sarah's Cottage, where he slid from his MV and, although unhurt, was unable to carry on.

A lap later the crowd hushed with the announcement that Hailwood had crashed at exactly the same spot, but was continuing. Mike kicked the MV straight, and pushing got the machine restarted, but the MV looking very second-hand, sporting a broken screen and flattened exhaust megaphones. His pit stop took 70 seconds as the mechanics straightened the bent handlebars and such, but he went on to win, at the slowest speed for six years, with Norton-mounted Joe Dunlop second and Mike Duff third on his Matchless.

And that was it for the first-generation MV fours. Hailwood defected to Honda and Agostini ran the new triple that would become a 500 four, but that would never come to the Isle of Man.

CHAPTER TEN

MV AGUSTA TRE CILINDRI

When the other big Italian factories withdrew from Grand Prix racing at the end of 1957, MV Agusta found they had the field to themselves – and then Honda came along. Honda's RC170, a 285cc version of their RC161 250 four, would quickly become the 1964 349.3cc RC172. Rather than see his sleeved-down 500 humiliated, Count Domenico withdrew from the

350 class and started afresh. To speed development a 350 triple was decided upon, built around a truncated 500 crankshaft.

Surprisingly to many this starting point was Domenico Agusta's idea. Although not an engineer, he would make suggestions to his team on sheets of paper in red pencil and expect those with greater training and experience than he

Giacomo Agostini's MV triple is a replica built by people with access to the original drawings and parts.

Agostini rounds Quarter Bridge in the 1971 Senior TT, a race he was expected to win easily before an unheard-of engine failure. TTRACEPICS.COM

had to make them work. The idea for the 3-cylinder – *il tre cilindri* – was then 'made beautiful', as the Count put it, by the manager of the drawing office, Mario Rossi, and his collaborators. Typically this office had a staff of five, rising to eight or nine when a major project was on. Of these draughtsmen only two actually had engineering degrees. Apart from these people and the qualified draughtsmen many were effectively self-taught, including MV's racing team manager, Arturo Magni. He worked on the project from the outset, for once giving up on brute power in favour of low weight, easy handling and minimal frontal area. The *tre cilindri* project started at the end

of 1963 with a simple brief: a new 350-class racing engine with 3-cylinders, to be as simple as possible, the crankshaft cut down from the 500cc four; separate cylinder heads; hair valve springs with an included valve angle of 91 degrees and two valves per cylinder (the norm at the time); dry clutch and 6- and 7-speed (depending on the track and conditions) cassette (i.e. removable) gearboxes; and the ignition system of the championship-winning 250cc twin. From here the team worked to provide a complete set of drawings by February 1964, the only departure from established norms being the external clutch.

At the 2013 Classic TT Pauline Hailwood waved off John McGuinness on a precise replica of Mike's RC181 Honda. Agostini rode with him to commemorate the 1967 Senior TT. IOMTT.COM/DAVE KNEEN/PACEMAKER PRESS

Early dynamometer testing was disappointing and the Count was not pleased. He discussed it with Mario Rossi, who had predicted the weak points of the new engine and ensured there were alternative drawings for a single-piece cylinder head with four valves per cylinder set at 73 degrees apart. After disappointment at the power from the two valve heads with traditional hemispherical combustion chambers – as on the old four – shallower 4-valve combustion chambers were decided upon, exactly the path Honda was pursuing. Bore and stroke were 52 x 54mm, giving 344cc. In August 1964 the new engine was bench-tested with this new head and triple 30mm Dell'Orto SSI carburettors. Power output was recorded at 63bhp at 13,500rpm and the bike was assembled with 35mm Ceriani GP forks and 18-inch wheels. Weight was 118kg (260lb).

The welded-up pressings that formed the box-section swinging arm was aircraft industry practice. The rear brake torque arm – a strip of aluminium alloy with rolled edges – looked suspiciously thin, but worked in tension so was fit for purpose, while weighing next to nothing. But where strength was important, it was there: a chunky eccentric swinging arm pivot for chain adjustment, and sturdy yokes with a large off-set. The brake drums might be MV's own, a Ceriani or an Oldani: all were used. The only instrument was a tachometer with a 4,000rpm starting point and a 12,300rpm redline, de-spite MV actually claiming maximum power arrived at over 13,000rpm. The frame, clinging tightly to the engine and in-unit gearbox, cleverly split in two: the bottom section and the engine just dropped to the floor. This was a far cry from period photos of Japanese bikes on their side, mechanics des-

Dean Harrison and the Kay replica MV Agusta of Black Eagle Racing during the Senior Classic TT. IOMTT.COM/DAVE KNEEN/PACEMAKER PRESS

perately trying to lever a motor free. In the days of constant carburation tweaking such things made a difference. Especially as MV tested a six-carburettor version.

This completed motorcycle was taken to Venice for Count Agusta to approve while he was holidaying there: it was run as a complete motorcycle for the first time on the streets of the Lido. The Count was apparently delighted. An Italian protégé who'd shown promise at Morini was then recruited for track testing: Giacomo Agostini.

Agostini and the triple had their World Championship debut at the 1965 German Grand Prix, which in those days meant the Nürburgring. Ironically this would be the very place Ago and MV would, in 1976, take the final Grand Prix victory for a 4-stroke before the arrival of MotoGP. The 1965 season opener had been at Daytona, only the second time there had been a US Grand Prix, and it would be 2007 before another was held. Effectively, then, the German round was the start of the 1965 season and Agostini's win there first time out served notice that Honda's dominance was at an end.

With no 350 or 500 race at the next two rounds in Spain and France, the big bikes returned to the fray on the Isle of Man. The Senior TT was a battle fought by the fours and principally MV's lead rider Mike Hailwood, but the Junior TT would be first time Agostini had raced on the mountain course. His debut was impressive. Jim Redman was chasing a hat-trick of consecutive Junior victories with the Honda four and Hailwood was determined to stop him. He set a new record on

his opening lap and led Redman by 20 seconds. By the third lap Hailwood had opened the gap to 28 seconds, but he then dropped back after a long pit stop. The pressure on the MV proved too great, and Hailwood retired at Sarah's Cottage on the fourth lap, leaving the way clear for Redman to achieve his goal. Phil Read was second on the Yamaha 2-stroke, with Agostini third after Derek Woodman went out on the last lap.

Redman triumphed at the next three rounds before a surprise win at the Ulster Grand Prix for Czech Frantisek Šastný. But then Ago took the wins in the next two rounds, and Hailwood the season finale in Japan, MV prepared to pay for Mike to fly out and compete in the 350 race, which he duly won. There was no 500 race, but Mike's win in the 350 class allowed him to claim third in the 350 championship for MV behind Ago and Honda's Redman, pushing Honda's Bruce Beale back into fourth. Ironically, the 250 race in Suzuka was Hailwood's first as a works Honda rider, and his first win for them.

1966 AND THE 371CC '500' MV AGUSTA TRE CILINDRI

With MV Agusta's 1965 500 champion Hailwood decamping to Honda for 1966, the Count demanded a bigger version of the triple to allow Agostini to fight for both the 350 and 500 championships. So once back in Italy at the end of the sea-

The replica MV triples are convincing and fast, but oddly not as reliable as the originals.

The narrower included valve angle of the triple is evident if you compare the cambox to that of the four.

son the team got to work on enlarging the 350 to make it a competitive mount for the 1966 500cc World Championship. The prototype triple had almost immediately had its capacity increased to 371cc with a 2mm increase in bore to 54mm, making the motor exactly square. This was another winner first time out at the Circuit of Modena on 20 March, with Alberto Pagani.

On the world stage Agostini started the year with the old four, and Honda's Jim Redman won the opening round of the 500cc World Championship at the West German Grand Prix at Hockenheim. MV therefore introduced a new '500' triple stretched to 400cc for the 1966 Dutch TT at Assen, Agostini immediately preferring the triple to the old 500 four. But Redman won again and looked to have the championship under control. And then Honda's hopes were dashed when Redman crashed in the rain in Belgium and broke his wrist, allowing Agostini to take the big triple to its first win.

By the East German round the triple's capacity was up to almost 420cc, bore increased to 57.4mm while stroke remained at 54mm. This was only the fourth outing in the nine-round 500cc championship but with only the five best results counting Agostini was already champion elect. Honda might have built an enviable reputation for reliability but Hailwood's challenge evaporated before it begun, with retirements in each of the first 500 rounds.

The East German Grand Prix was won by Štastný on a Jawa CZ, but behind him was a battle royal between Hailwood and Agostini. The season rattled on in a similar vein: if Hailwood won Agostini would be second, and vice versa. Eventually Agostini won the final round at Monza while Hailwood and Honda suffered another ignominious retirement.

The Isle of Man TT had actually been the penultimate round of the 500cc championship in 1966, postponed until September because of a seamen's strike. So this would be the first time British enthusiasts had witnessed the Hailwood/Honda–Agostini/MV battle they had only read of in a breathless and partisan press at first hand, and they were not to be disappointed.

The 500cc 4-cylinder Honda was a brute and not the ideal machine for the mountain course, with the smaller Japanese bikes not much better. But Mike tamed them all with a display of skill and bravery that was the hallmark of a true champion, in the 250 and 350cc classes at least.

Hailwood and Agostini had started TT week with the six-lap Junior, but the struggle lasted just a few miles until Hailwood's Honda ground to a halt at Bishopscourt on the very first lap, leaving the way clear for Agostini and the MV. But that didn't stop the Italian setting a new class record on his second lap of 103.09mph (165.87km/h) on the way to a comfortable maiden TT victory.

The Senior at the end of the week was what the TT fans wanted to see most. A lap record from a standing start gave first blood to Hailwood, but Agostini wasn't giving up without a fight. On the second lap it was his turn to take the lap record in a valiant effort to keep the Honda in sight. Hailwood increased the record yet again on lap three to lead his neme-

McGuinness and Agostini complete the parade lap. Agostini joked that his chain broke again (as it did in 1967) but that McGuiness stopped and helped him fix it.

The television crew includes James Whitham but the dog's not impressed.

sis by 13 seconds. He then gradually pulled away to secure his ninth and perhaps most impressive TT victory. Agostini was a brilliant second, with RAF Corporal Chris Conn completing a perfect week by finishing third on his Norton.

So Agostini took the greatest prize motorcycle racing can offer at only his second attempt, up against the might of Honda and the brilliance of Hailwood. In truth the issue was down to reliability as much as anything else, and presumably many heads rolled back in Japan as a result of these very public failings. What further tribulations would have been visited on these unfortunate souls if Honda knew they'd been beaten by a bike that had started with only 400cc to their full 500cc, we can never know.

Of course MV's team knew that they must get to that full capacity as quickly as possible, and by the end of the year the motor was seriously oversquare with the bore up to 62mm and stroke held at 54mm to give 488.9cc. For 1967 they would test the concept further, going to 66 x 48.6mm to achieve 498.9cc. Breathing through three 31mm Dell'Orto SS1 carburettors and with an 11:1 compression ratio, power was up to 88bhp at 13,000rpm.

1967 RERUNS 1966 – AND THE GREATEST SENIOR TT EVER?

The new season was pretty much a rerun of 1966, with almost every round a win for either Hailwood or Ago and a second place if not. Mike suffered three retirements to Agostini's one, but a disastrous Ulster Grand Prix left Ago out of the points when Hailwood took victory.

It was the TT's Diamond Jubilee Year, with the event back in its traditional June slot. By now everybody knew Honda was withdrawing from motorcycle racing at the end of the season and were paying Hailwood for an agreement that he would not join another team. So while everybody was happy to celebrate the sixtieth anniversary of the first TT race, it was tinged with sadness because all thought it would be Hailwood's last races on the island.

In the Junior TT, aboard the 296cc 6-cylinder Honda, Hailwood was in a class of his own. He destroyed the absolute lap record from a standing start at a speed of 107.73mph (173.34km/h) and continued at almost the same pace, only dropping his speed towards the end of

Races can be won or lost in a pit stop, which remains mandatory.

the six laps. Nobody, not even Agostini in a comfortable second place, could stay with him.

But it was Hailwood's duel with Agostini in the Diamond Jubilee Senior that is still regarded by many as the greatest TT race of all time. Friday arrived and the often fickle Isle of Man weather was as perfect as it could be. The tension was palpable. The long line of starters stretched back along Glencrutchery Road towards Governor's Bridge.

Hailwood started at number four, and thirty seconds later Agostini took up the chase. Agostini destroyed the lap record from a standing start, breaking the 21-minute barrier with a speed of 108.38mph (174.38km/h), to lead by 11.8 seconds. Obviously not happy with the handling of the Honda, Mike gave a 'thumbs down' as he screamed through to start his second lap.

It was not all Agostini and Hailwood. Renzo Pasolini lapped at 100.06mph (161km/h) from a standing start on the Benelli four and then a British machine also topped the ton when Peter Williams' Arter Matchless lapped at 100.35mph (161.46km/h).

Up at the front, Hailwood had realized from his pit board that he needed to up his pace if he was to win and started inching away from Agostini. It was a supreme effort, the Honda literally bouncing from bump to bump as he wrestled with it to end his second lap with another record – 108.77mph (175.01km/h) – that would stand until 1975. Yet still Agostini led the race, albeit with his advantage cut to 8.6 seconds. After three laps both Hailwood and Agostini were averaging over 108mph (173.77km/h) and the grandstand burst into a feeding frenzy as fans pushed to see how the critical pit stops would go. As Agostini and then Hailwood came in, Hailwood having cut the lead down to two seconds, but he toured into the pits slowly.

'Get me a hammer' he yelled as the mechanics started to refuel the Honda. The twist grip had been slipping off the handlebar, Mike hammering it back into place before pulling down his goggles and roaring off once more. The stop lasted 47.8 seconds, costing Hailwood a full 10 seconds. Agostini now led by 15 seconds, and the fight was well and truly joined.

Having to hold the loose throttle in place and use sheer

Attention to detail is a hallmark of the original and replica triples.

brute force to keep the Honda between the hedges and walls, incredibly Hailwood managed to once again reel in Agostini. At the start of the fifth lap the gap was 11.6 seconds. At Ramsey it was reported that Hailwood led by a single second, his board signalling station there held up '–6': minus six seconds, still giving Agostini the lead.

By now Agostini was aware he was being caught and turned the wick up yet again, with timing at the Bungalow placing him 2.5 seconds in the lead. Then, as Hailwood screamed past the scoreboard for his final lap, Agostini's allocated scoreboard light did not come on to indicate he had passed Signpost Corner. Finally the news reached the grandstand – he had stopped on the mountain with a broken chain. A groan went up from the crowd – the race was over.

Although he saw the signals from the spectators indicating that Agostini had retired, Hailwood pressed on until he reached Ramsey, where he saw the good news on a pit board held up by mechanic Nobby Clark, and he toured home, holding onto his loose throttle. Once off the bike Hailwood told the press:

I was lucky. If Ago's chain hadn't broken, I don't think I could have won. That second lap was just about as fast as I could go. I made up quite a bit of time, but lost it at the pit stop when I had to fix the throttle.

It started to work loose again on the fifth lap, and on the last lap I was riding virtually one handed. In fact I almost had to stop once to push it back on again and was holding it for most of the lap.

It was Hailwood's twelfth TT win and his third that week, including the 250 race, a repeat of his 1961 performance.

At the end of the year Hailwood and Agostini had 46 points each from their best six performances, so the rules required counting back on other finishes. On the basis that, if all rounds were counted, Agostini would have been awarded 58 points to Hailwood's 52, Giacomo Agostini was declared the 1967 500cc World Champion. Mike and Honda's consolation prizes were the 250 and 350 titles, Ago the runner-up in the latter.

With Honda gone and Agostini armed with a bike built to beat the best the Japanese could build and then have ridden by Hailwood, 1968 was the predicted clean sweep. Agostini and his magnificent MVs won every 350 and 500 race of the year, a feat almost repeated every year until 1973.

A FATALITY TOO FAR

But it was in 1972 that MV Agusta and the Isle of Man TT parted company. One fatality in particular marked a sea change in the TT's reputation and kicked off a fall from grace that made it seem inevitable that the TT would, like every other road course race in the history books, disappear forever. After winning the first two 125cc Grand Prix races of the 1972 season, Italian Gilberto Parlotti and his equally Italian Morbidelli team decided to race at the Isle of Man. At this time the TT was still the British Grand Prix and, with World Championship points on the table, few riders dared miss it. Taking advantage of his main championship rival Angel Nieto's absence, Parlotti led the Ultra Lightweight TT, looking like the champion elect and ready to gift Morbidelli an historic world title.

Chas Mortimer, who had won his first TT race two years previously aboard a Ducati 250 was initially race favourite,

setting off immediately before Parlotti on a Yamaha. Unlike other riders who had questioned how the race could be started in the very wet conditions, Mortimer felt he could win at a pace he felt comfortable with. But when he arrived at Ramsey his board read '−10' (ten seconds behind the leader) he upped the pace across the mountain, only to find he was now twelve seconds adrift of the lead.

Of course the leader was Parlotti seemingly a racing certainty for his debut TT win and an increased lead in the 125cc World Championship. But the fog and heavy rain created increasingly treacherous conditions and an alternative, horrific, reality unfolded. While leading comfortably, Parlotti crashed at Veranda on the second lap. His injuries proved fatal.

Depending on who you believe – or perhaps both stories are true – the Parlotti family's friend Count Agusta simply refused to allow his MV motorcycles to return to the Isle of Man. And Gilberto's close friend Giacomo Agostini initially said he wouldn't race in the Senior TT at the end of the week, although he was eventually persuaded to do so. But while 1972's TT week continued, Agostini vowed he would never return, declaring it too dangerous to be a part of the FIM World Championship. At the time Ago was undoubtedly

Note eccentric swing arm pivot for chain adjustment, something John Surtees initiated on the Quattro.

Four laps and that many flies on the fairing.

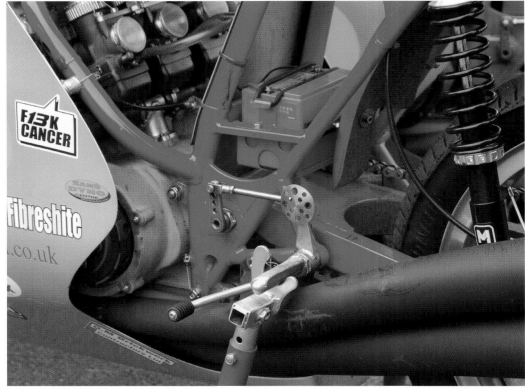

Even the rose joint's guard is drilled to save weight.

the most popular – and successful – motorcycle racer in the world, and was probably the only rider who could have made such a threat convincingly.

The ACU and FIM initially were sure that riders would drift back to the TT, and that factories would force their hand. But when the new breed of superstar riders, notably Barry Sheene, joined Agostini's boycott, the writing was on the wall. For 1973 it was agreed that if weather conditions prevented the rescue helicopter from flying then races would be delayed or cancelled but it was too little, too late. For 1976, the TT was dropped from the World Championship calendar, and the British Grand Prix moved to Silverstone. The Isle of Man was awarded the inaugural Formula TT races – nominally a single-round World Championship – as a sweetener, but nobody seriously expected racing on the Isle of Man to survive.

WHAT THE TRE CILINDRI WAS LIKE TO RIDE

From 1966 to 1973 Agostini used the triple to win six 350 and seven 500 World Championships. Away from the TT, his new team-mate Phil Read then used the triple to take the 1973 500 World Championship, but by now more power was needed. The 350 triple evolved into a 500 four that lost some of the

sweet handling of the triple in the process, especially with the heavy 16-valve head. Nonetheless, Read would take a second championship with the bike. I have been fortunate enough to discuss the bikes with Phil and these were his thoughts:

The MV's were good bikes, but they could have been so much better. It was only when Jarno [Saarinen, with Yamaha] came along that things started to change. Jarno was winning, sometimes by five or six seconds a lap. Magni had been there since Surtees' days and seemed to think they could just carry on doing what they'd always done. We really needed more lateral thinking, someone to bring in new ideas. The silly thing is the Agusta helicopter factory was just up the road with some of the best minds and equipment in the world. [Yet looking over the MV does reveal aerospace engineering, such as the welded up pressings that form the box section swinging arm were aircraft industry practice – author.]

They should have been trying [disc brakes] but they just stuck a big Oldani on with green linings. Now I've got those on my Moto Paton, and they're very powerful, but you've got to put quite a serious taper on the leading edge before bedding them in. About the first time I went out on the 500 I just touched the brake lever, the wheel locked, and down I went. They were brand new linings, not tapered or bedded in, but just fitted and handed over.

The winner's enclosure proves the MV's success rate.

The 350 three was tested with six carburettors, but I think it got tried once at Monza and forgotten. The magnesium monoblock carbs were pretty good, mind you. But then you had the rear sprocket so far from the swinging arm pivot, meaning that chain pull left you with hardly any suspension accelerating hard out of corners – and the roads were a lot bumpier back then. [Less chain pull might also have saved Ago's pride in 1967 – author] The MV was a much better bike than the Honda [500 RC181]: manoeuvrability was so good, and it had good acceleration out of corners with plenty of torque; it could just drive away from the peakier 2-strokes. But of course the Japanese kept on developing them, which is why we needed to go back to a four: that had 100 to101 horsepower from the start, where the three was around 85. That's still actually more than the replica Giacomo's got, and that was unreliable to start with. The original was bulletproof.

It is often written that the MV racing department lost its influence with the Agusta family when Count Domenico died in 1971. In fact his successor, Count Corrado, brought in Giuseppe Bocchi from Ferrari to design a replacement for the racing fours. He designed and built a flat-four 500 with liquid cooling and fuel injection. It was lighter, lower, more compact and much more powerful than the old inline four. Agostini and Read have both told me that the problem was trying to get Magni and Bocchi to cooperate, but there was a further complication.

Despite what is commonly believed, MV almost always had more power that their 2-stroke rivals but carried more weight, which affected acceleration and handling. It was the noise restrictions that the FIM imposed in 1976 that hurt MV and later Honda's NR500, because silencers robbed 4-strokes of more power than they did 2-strokes. The rules gave existing designs a few years' grace, which is why the old 350 was wheeled out for the German Grand Prix at the Nürburgring Sudschleife in 1976, to take the final Grand Prix World Championship victory for a 4-stroke before the arrival of MotoGP.

In the end MV won the 500 constructors' title every year from 1958 until 1973. They might have done the same with the 350 championship, but walked away from the class for a good chunk of the 1960s. Depending on who you ask this was either because they feared being beaten by Honda, or to make sure they could beat Honda in the 500 class. Even so, for a team of people that numbered perhaps a dozen including riders working for a factory that only ever built a few hundred thousand motorcycles it was an incredible achievement.

Michael Dunlop at speed on the MV Agusta during Classic TT qualifying. IOMTT.COM/DAVE KNEEN/PACEMAKER PRESS

CHAPTER ELEVEN

THE JAPANESE ARRIVE BEARING 2-STROKES

Although they might seem indistinguishable now – giant Japanese corporations racing large-capacity motorcycles to sell mopeds in emerging markets – in the beginning, the Japanese factories each had a very particular character. Kawasaki had a huge industrial base, having started out as a ship builder. Suzuki built looms and Yamaha, musical instruments. All were large businesses looking to diversify, and they fell upon motorcycles. Honda alone was the vision of one man who wanted to build motorcycles, and the best motorcycles in the world at that. Soichiro Honda was the first of the Japanese to appreciate the special challenges and opportunities of the Isle of Man TT, and the first to conquer it. He also hated 2-strokes, as well as water cooling.

The other Japanese factories were more pragmatic, especially after Ernst Degner defected and sold Walter Kaaden's hard-won secrets to Suzuki. Everyone else had believed that, without supercharging, a 2-stroke could never compete with a 4-stroke, despite having one power stroke for every two rotations of the crankshaft: you simply couldn't exercise enough control without the 4-stroke's valves that allowed precision in the suck–squeeze–bang–blow cycle that meant a 4-stroke could only offer one power stroke for every four turns of the crankshaft.

EAST GERMANS TEACH SUZUKI THEIR MOST VALUABLE LESSON

But Kaaden realized you could use crankcase compression, sucking air into the crankcases as a piston rose on the exhaust stroke and then transferring it into the cylinder as the piston fell: the piston both sucked the charge in as well as forced it

Early Honda 125 shows how the look of the NSU twins influenced Soichiro Honda after his first TT visit.

Yamaha's YD1 250 shows how early on an engine template was formed, although the styling was odd to Western eyes. PEKEPON

A 1965 Suzuki T20 shows – as with Yamaha – a motor that shares a look with much later models. RAINMAKER 47

A 1968 Kawasaki Avenger A7, popular in the US but rare in the UK. RAINMAKER 47

into the cylinder as the underside of the piston squeezed it. Years later the FIM admitted this should have been banned as a form of supercharging, but initially they shied away from penalising Kaaden's tiny MZ team. Once the genie was out of the bottle (unlike the 2-stroke's crankcase compression…) there was no way to squeeze it back in.

Kaaden's genius was controlling all of this without a 4-stroke's valve gear, instead using a rotary disc valve between the carburettor and the crankcase, and an expansion chamber to reflect shock waves created by combustion back towards the cylinder and so prevent most of the fresh charge from escaping through the exhaust port. Kaaden achieved astounding success, given his lack of resources, but once his ideas were in the hands of Suzuki there was no stopping the rise of the 2-stroke. Once this was perfected, the only way a 4-stroke

could compete was to spin twice as fast, assuming you could overcome the problems that brought, such as reciprocating mass, which meant making the parts of an engine that go up and down much smaller. This was Honda's method, using smaller pistons but more of them. Once the 500cc Grand Prix motorcycles were limited to 4-cylinders and six gears in 1969 that possibility evaporated, although Honda tried to circumvent it with the 'oval'-pistoned NR500.

The alternative was to allow the 4-strokes to have twice the capacity, which is what the FIM eventually did when they created MotoGP, breaking the tradition of 500cc motorcycle racing being the pinnacle of the sport. 2-strokes remained limited to 500cc while the 4-strokes were allowed 990cc and one hegemony was replaced with another. It seems a shame when you realize how different it once was.

CHAPTER TWELVE

HONDA RC181

It is slightly odd that many motorcycle fans can be slightly sniffy about Hondas. Of course they have their fans. but often these are interested in a particular model, typically the 400 Four or the magnificent RC30 VFR750R. Terms such as 'bland', 'characterless' and 'UJM' (Universal Japanese Motorcycle) are applied. If only they knew more about the marque's eponymous founder, Soichiro Honda, a man who rose from nothing to become a very powerful, very eccentric, maverick who built the world's biggest motorcycle manufacturer from nothing. A man whose idea of a good Saturday night out was to put on one of his beloved red shirts, climb into his Cadillac convertible and drive Geisha girls around Tokyo before taking them to dinner. A man who would explain to fellow engineers that they were wrong by coming at them with a weaponized spanner. A man so opposed to 2-strokes that when he came across the prototype NS500 triple he was told it was for a lawnmower. A man so opposed to liquid cooling – as was Ducati's Fabio Taglioni – that it would eventually lead to his retirement from the main board.

Soichiro Honda was not a man who liked academics. He left school at 15 with his parents blissfully unaware that he had forged the family stamp so that he could return school reports to teachers without showing them to anyone. He only hung onto his first job at a Tokyo garage because he was one of the few who didn't flee after an earthquake. But gradually the drive that would make him great started to show. He had his own garage at 22 and by 1937 a successful business making piston rings for Toyota. After the war they bought him out and Honda used the money to bolt war-surplus generators onto bicycles that a nation desperate for transport bought as fast as he could build them.

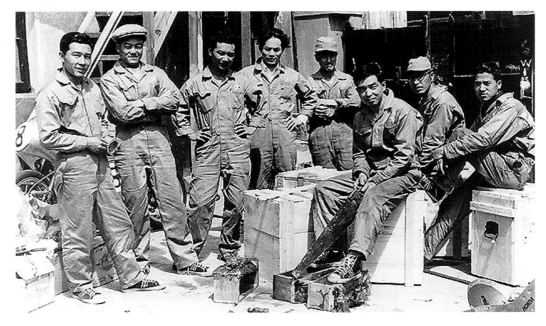

The Honda team at their first-ever TT in 1959.
HONDA MOTOR CORPORATION

Naomi Taniguchi on the RC142 at the 1959 Ultra Lightweight (125) TT. He finished sixth, the first Honda home. HONDA MOTOR CORPORATION

In 1948 the Honda Motor Company was born with his new business partner and trusted friend, Takeo Fujisawa. Honda-san was to be product development and Fujisawa-san brought the necessary business nous. The pair set up shop as a motorcycle manufacturer with thirty-four employees. The Americans were cheerfully running around Japan trying to make sure the country didn't follow most of its near neighbours into communism by offering almost anybody with a business plan 'soft' loans: in effect, loans that the US government didn't really expect to be repaid. Honda's first factory was built on a slope with the production line running downhill to speed things up.

The first Honda motorcycle, the 1949 D-Type, was a 2-stroke to keep costs down, but Soichiro's fervent belief in 4-strokes soon brought the 1951 Dream E with a 146cc ohv motor.

SOICHIRO HONDA'S VISION STRIKES A CHORD

And then something extraordinary happened that brought a flood of people wanting to work with Honda. He published

The RC160 from 1959, a dohc 250cc four-cylinder racer. Note the deeply treaded tyres for racing on rough tracks in Japan. HONDA MOTOR CORPORATION

an essay in 1952, 'The beauty and artistry of products', that today we would say went viral. 'Although Japan's machinery industries have fallen completely behind the west, I feel the calling to create motorcycles. More than anything else I want to create utterly beautiful shapes that are in no way inferior to those produced in other countries' gives an insight into Honda's beliefs and ambitions.

To future-proof Honda, the man took himself off to Europe, determined to learn from the best. He was planning the 2-cylinder 250 and 305 Dreams and had visions of racing them on the Isle of Man. Therefore the 1954 TT was one of his first stops – and his first big shock. The course – even the shorted Clypse course sometimes then used for the smaller bikes – staggered him as it does most first-time visitors. And, while Honda had pencilled in a target

of 10bhp for his first 250, the NSU 4-stroke twins that were dominating the 250cc Lightweight TT had almost four times that.

Years later, Honda admitted he had almost given up there and then, and flown home. (Honda would become the largest motorcycle manufacturer in Japan in 1955, so it would hardly have been giving up in most people's eyes!) It is a mark of the man that not only did he continue his tour but that he became ever more determined that Honda would succeed in the World Championship. Clothes were discarded as his suitcases filled with Avon racing tyres, Reynolds chains, Borrani rims and Dell'Orto carburettors on his way to Rome and his flight home.

Pretty much leaving Fujisawa in charge, Honda established a secret camp to develop a 125cc 2-cylinder racer for the

The 3RC164, the 250 six-cylinder racer of 1964. HONDA MOTOR CORPORATION

1959 TT. His co-conspirator was a young engineer, Kiyoshi Kawashima, and their project codename was RC141. 2-cylinders would allow the motor to spin faster than the European singles and so potentially give more power. Kawashima reckoned on 18bhp being competitive, but Honda wasn't so sure, especially when the bike was trounced in its first races in Japan. Honda knew that a 'competitive' European racer would simply hit the front of the pack before disappearing into the distance against existing Japanese motorcycles. So, when he heard that the Italians were abandoning Grand Prix racing at the end of 1957, Honda wrote to the Fratelli brothers, who owned Mondial, to ask if he might buy one of their dominant 125 singles.

MONDIAL SHOW HONDA THE WAY

Mondial had form on this, having sold a 125 to MV Agusta who used it to build a bike that could beat Mondial's. So of course Mondial agreed to supply Honda with a 125 single, the first bike you see on entering the Honda museum. It is also the reason that the only time Honda have agreed to supply an engine to another motorcycle manufacturer was when there was a doomed attempt to revive the marque with the VTR-powered Piega in 2003.

Kawashima was horrified when the diminutive Mondial arrived, a three-year-old single-cylinder design that gave almost 10 per cent more power than Honda's twin. He immediately set about designing 4-valve heads, although

The TV crew admire the very convincing replica of Mike Hailwood's 1967 RC181. Mike's son, David, is on the right.

reliability concerns meant they weren't initially shipped out to the Isle of Man.

HONDA'S FIRST TT

Honda arrived on the island in 1959 with five riders and nine bikes, plus enough spares and tools to create a self-sufficient workshop. The bikes were brought over with two valves per cylinder but, during practice, it became clear that the bikes were lacking in power and the 4-valve heads were flown in from Japan. The bikes would finish 6th, 7th, 8th and 11th, with one rider crashing out, earning Honda the team prize. The Ultra Lightweight TT might have been run on the less challenging Clypse course that didn't include Snaefell, but it proved that the Honda's were reliable. Some European manufacturers comforted themselves with the Hondas' lack of speed, but the results no doubt would have been better with riders

Even a replica of an RC181 costs as much as a nice house, so the Classic TT racers are based on the sohc road bike motors.

better acquainted with the TT course. Honda must have spent as much on this one trip as most factories would spend on an entire season.

Honda also unveiled a 250cc 4-cylinder racer in 1959, although it was hardly a new idea in itself. Before the war Gilera, Bianchi and Benelli had all built supercharged 250 fours, the Benelli water-cooled, the other two air-cooled. As we have seen, supercharged designs struggled when denied forced induction and it was only in 1960, a year after the Honda four was introduced, that Benelli again fielded a 250cc four.

The Honda four, designated the RC160, was never raced outside of Japan and, because those races were often on unpaved roads, was mostly shown without a fairing and with deeply treaded tyres.

4-CYLINDER AMBITIONS AND THE UNIVERSAL JAPANESE MOTORCYCLE

The arrival of a 4-cylinder Honda is important. Soichiro, on his tour of Europe, had noted that marques often had a defining engine layout: BMWs were flat twins, the British had vertical singles and parallel twins, Moto Guzzi the horizontal single, Harley-Davidson the narrow V-twin. Honda decided that his factory would be associated with inline fours, only turning to more than that if absolutely necessary. Once that association was made in the public mind, Honda would launch their own range of road-going fours. The fury in the boardroom and of Honda personally when Kawasaki followed them and the term UJM (Universal Japanese Motorcycle) was coined by

Mike Hailwood with the RC181 in 1967. HONDA MOTOR CORPORATION

American journalist Phil Schilling cannot be underestimated. Schilling used the UJM jibe when testing the Kawasaki Z650 four shortly after Suzuki had launched their near-identical GS750. It would drive Honda into building V4s, again at the suggestion of Schilling and his editor Cook Neilson, ironically at the launch of the 6-cylinder CBX.

So for 1966 Honda abandoned the glorious 6-cylinder racers and brought out brand new 350 and 500 fours. At this point it is worth mentioning that Honda didn't always go racing just to win, but rather to learn. The engineers were usually brought in at the beginning of their careers and often with an aeronautical rather that mechanical engineering degree. This was notably true of Shoichiro Irimajiri, eventual head of Honda's research and development and the man who led the design teams for both the racing sixes and the later road-going CBX six.

And Honda would never buy components in, apparently happy to learn from their mistakes. Mike Hailwood once fa-

mously threw Honda's rear shock absorbers over a hedge, desperate for some British Girlings. Later on, when running the NR500 project, Gerald Davidson was frustrated when components were used that weren't a patch on what he could buy off the shelf in Italy. He told the author that 'I'd be promised the best throttle ever designed and I'd say "Oh, really? What were you working on before?" and the answer would be something like "oh, front wings for the car division"'. Honda believed that this approach would create original thinkers and new solutions, but it was a source of friction with those trying to win races.

And so to the all-new 4-cylinder racer for 1966, the 350cc RC173, developed alongside the 500cc RC181. The bikes were virtually identical, but there were small differences: the RC173 had round camshaft covers, the RC181 rectangular ones. Both engines were wet-sump designs with external oil coolers and 6-speed integral gearboxes. The 350's bore and

John McGuinness, dressed to recall Mike Hailwood's 1967 Senior TT win, pushes off with Giacomo Agostini. IOMTT.COM/DAVE KNEEN/PACEMAKER PRESS

stroke was Honda's tried-and-tested 50 × 44.5mm, giving 64bhp at 13,000rpm. The frames had bolted-on, twin front down-tubes, not unlike the MV's and far removed from the pressed-steel items Honda started out with, probably inspired by the NSU 250s that Soichiro Honda had seen on his first visit to the TT.

The 500cc RC181 was even more oversquare than its sibling at 57 × 48mm bore and stroke, giving a total capacity of 489.94cc. Included valve angle (four per cylinder, of course) was a comparatively narrow 75 degrees, showing the way for the future of four-stoke design, and a lesson that MV had only just learnt. Power output was 85bhp at 12,000rpm, with a redline at 12,500rpm. Dry weight was 151kg (333lb), a fair lump of metal and almost 30 per cent more than the MV triple.

The weak point of the RC181 would prove to be its crankshaft, the press fit sometimes giving up with disastrous results: this was the reason for Hailwood's retirement in the

final round of the World Championship at Monza. Attempts to improve handling included mounting the front axle in an eccentric, allowing trail to be altered. Hailwood would rather have had Girling rear shock absorbers.

The nature of the 1966 and 1967 season's duelling between Agostini on the MVs and Hailwood on the Hondas means that much of the RC181's story is told in the previous chapter. In the 1966 500cc World Championship Hailwood retired from the first four rounds of the 500 championship as well as the final outing at Monza, while Agostini suffered a single DNF. When both riders finished it would be in first or second place, with each garnering three wins. Hailwood of course took the 350 title, the 350 Honda 4-cylinder RC173 proving more reliable and manageable than the RC181. But it was a close-fought battle.

The TT was the penultimate round of the 1966 World Championship, a seamen's strike earlier in the year forcing it

ABOVE: **After the parade lap McGuinness discusses the Hailwood replica with its owner.**

James Whitham interviews Agostini about his memories of the 1967 Senior TT.

to be moved from its traditional June date. This was the time British fans had seen the Hailwood and Honda versus Agostini and MV battle in the flesh, and they were not disappointed. Hailwood and Agostini were first out in the six-lap Junior, the Italian winning his first TT. The struggle lasted just a few miles until Hailwood's Honda ground to a halt at Bishopscourt on the very first lap, leaving the way clear for Agostini and the MV triple.

The Senior that closed the event on 2 September was the real treat. The 500cc 4-cylinder Honda was an animal when ridden at a pace that might allow a race win and hardly the ideal machine for the mountain course. But Mike tamed it with a display of skill and bravery that was the hallmark of a true champion even if he wouldn't be in the 500cc class. A new lap record from a standing start gave first blood to Hailwood, although Agostini was far from beaten. On the second lap the Italian raised the lap record again to keep the mighty Honda in sight. Hailwood pushed the record to 107.07mph (172.28km/h) on lap 3 to lead his rival by 13 seconds. Mike then gradually pulled away to secure his ninth – and arguably his greatest – TT victory. Agostini was second, as he always was when he didn't win. The season ended with Agostini on 36 points to Hailwood's 30, but it wasn't as close as it looked. The final tally was still only taken from best five results in 350cc and 500cc championships, despite there being nine rounds. If, as today, every round has counted, Agostini would have collected 54 points, getting on for twice Mike's haul.

MINOR REVISIONS TO THE RC181 FOR 1967

Over the winter Honda revised the 500, but not by much. Most of Honda's racing department was preparing for Honda's push to win the Formula 1 car racing World Championship the following season. So for 1967, still designated The RC181, the bolted on sub-frame was welded up in a search for better handling and the megaphones lost the reverse cones for more power. Capacity increased to 499.7cc by enlarging the bore by half a millimetre. Power output was claimed to be up by 5bhp to 90bhp at 12,000rpm, with maximum torque at 10,000rpm. Mike Hailwood reputedly asked the Honda crew when they arrived in Europe at the start of the 1967 season if they'd improved the handling of the RC181. The response was apparently an inscrutable 'Mike-san we have another five horsepower for you.'

Given that Honda was abandoning motorcycle racing to focus on car racing the following year, for 1967 the motorcycle engineers had been told to focus on finding power, seeking out ideas transferable to the Formula 1 team. This meant that the motorcycles' chassis received little or no development. Infamously Hailwood took a dim view of this and, while he had to ride what Honda provided at World Championship races, at other events he would indulge his interest in development. The first innovation involved a man most will never have heard of: independent engineer Colin Lyster. He effec-

The real thing – Hailwood and the Honda RC181 in action. HONDA MOTOR CORPORATION

Convincing and competitive, the RC181 replica.

tively invented disc brakes for motorcycles, developing a set-up built around Ceriani forks during the mid-1960s. Mike was one of the first to try these, having them fitted to his 500cc 4-cylinder RC181. After failing to convince the British motor-cycle industry of their worth, Lyster sold his patents to AP Lockheed and went back to frame building and his dream of building a 500cc Grand Prix racer powered by half a Hillman Imp engine.

A NEW FRAME – BUT NOT WHERE IT WAS NEEDED

Mike also asked Lyster if he could make him a frame, which he could only agree to if Hailwood would wait two months. This was too long, so Hailwood contacted Pep Pattoni, co-found-er with Lino Tonti of Paton. Hailwood had raced with Paton and remembered their frames were welded by a specialist company in Milan. This was Officina Belletti, and Stelio Belletti worked with Lino Tonti to create a new rolling chassis for Mike. It was only ever used at non-championship events and Honda turned a blind eye on the proviso that Hailwood did not tell the press about it.

The same search for power influenced Hailwood's '350' entry. The 4-cylinder, 64bhp, 350cc RC173 was replaced by

the RC174, an enlarged version of the RC166 250 six, the capacity of 297.06cc achieved by retaining the bore of 41mm and increasing stroke to 37.5mm. With a compression ratio of 10.6:1 and six 22mm carburettors, power output was given as 67bhp at a dizzying 17,000rpm, with maximum torque at 16,000rpm.

1967 would be a seminal year in motorcycle Grand Prix history as well as the end of an era, with Honda deciding to withdraw from competition in the motorcycle World Cham-pionships. Nevertheless, Honda would go out with a bang, with Mike Hailwood taking the 250 and 350cc crowns and coming within a whisker of dethroning Giacomo Agostini for the 500cc title. In the 250cc class Phil Read would battle Hail-wood mightily for the title. They finished the season with 50 points apiece, but Hailwood took the title because he had five wins to Read's four. In the 350 class Hailwood had an easier time, taking six wins and claiming the crown by mid-season.

A MAGNIFICENT CHAMPIONSHIP BATTLE

The 500 title fight would be one for the history books with Agostini and Hailwood swapping wins back and forth includ-ing the legendary duel at the Isle of Man Senior TT. The chase

Soichiro Honda's dream was for the buying public to see a 4-cylinder 4-stroke motorcycle, be it a racer or a road bike such as this CB750, and assume it was a Honda.

HONDA MOTOR CORPORATION

went down to the last race in Canada. Hailwood won there to tie Agostini on points. Each rider had five wins so it came down to second places. Agostini snatched the title with three second places to Hailwood's two.

With Honda leaving the motorcycle Grand Prix championships in 1968 Hailwood left motorcycle racing to resume his car-racing career. Mike had first dabbled in Formula 1 racing in 1963, making a serious attempt at the title in 1964– the year John Surtees lifted the title – driving a Reg Parnell Racing Lotus 25 with a BRM engine. Mike competed in nine of the ten rounds, only missing the Belgium round at Spa on the 14 June because it clashed with the TT.

Diamond Jubilee Year and Mike Hailwood celebrated the sixtieth anniversary of the first TT race – and what everybody thought would be his last appearance on the Island – with a magnificent trio of wins aboard the works Hondas. His duel with Agostini in the Diamond Jubilee Senior is still regarded by many as the greatest TT race of all time. Hailwood had started his record-breaking week by winning the Lightweight (250cc) TT, although Read and Ivy worked desperately hard to spoil his party.

In the Junior TT, riding the 296cc 6-cylinder Honda, Hailwood was in a class of one. He decimated the absolute lap

record – usually set with a 500 – from a standing start at a speed of 107.73mph (173.34km/h) and continued at nearly the same pace, not dropping his speed until near the end of the six laps. Nobody, not even Agostini, could stay with him. Agostini was a comfortable second from Derek Woodman on the 2-stroke MZ.

Hailwood departed World Championship motorcycle racing in a blaze of glory, victorious in three classes in one day at the Dutch TT as well as three classes in one week on the Isle of Man. The first win at the 1967 TT gave Hailwood his tenth TT victory, equalling Stanley Woods's record. His two wins later in the week made him the most successful TT rider of all time with twelve wins – the reason for 12 being his race number on the Ducati 900F1 he won his next TT on in 1978. The record would stand until Ulsterman Joey Dunlop equalled and then passed Mike's record in 1992 and 1993, respectively.

When Honda quit motorcycle Grand Prix racing at the end of the 1967 season everyone assumed Mike was lost to the Island forever. The man was to prove them wrong eleven long years later, when he returned with a fleet of Yamahas that were expected to propel him to glory. But it was the Ducati win that took the headlines, and was the ultimate chapter in the Mike Hailwood legend.

CHAPTER THIRTEEN

YAMAHA TZ350

In 1887 Torakusu Yamaha, the son of an astronomer and a trained watchsmith, started making reed organs and, twelve years later under the Nippon Gakki banner, moved on to pianos. The piano business was financially lucrative, but in the 1920s sales were hit by the rising popularity of radio as the home entertainment of choice. Piano manufacture continued but, to maintain overall profitability, the firm diversified into manufacturing high-quality aircraft parts using the Yamaha name and the famous triple tuning fork logo.

Yamaha made its iron piano frames by sand casting and the keys were pressure-cast in aluminium alloy and then coated in plastic. Yamaha was a world leader in these technologies and, after World War II, was approached by motorcycle manufacturers to make castings. In 1954 Yamaha decided to start on its own two-wheelers.

In 1955 the Yamaha Motor Company was established as a separate enterprise with its own factory and a workforce of less than 100. The first Yamaha motorcycle was the YA1, re-

Hailwood with the six-cylinder RC166 eyes Phil Read and the Yamaha 250 in 1967. HONDA MOTOR CORPORATION

leased in 1955, greatly influenced by DKW's pre-war 2-stroke single and so looking very much like a BSA Bantam (which had been influenced by DKW plans confiscated as reparations after World War II). But, unlike the Bantam, Yamaha's version of the 125cc single featured substantial improvements over the German original and this, alongside an exhaustive testing programme, resulted in a strong and reliable motorcycle. The motorcycle was an immediate hit with the Japanese public and became known as the 'Red Dragonfly', although it was actually painted maroon and cream.

Yamaha quickly became involved in competition events, and the YA1 and its successors were victorious in the hotly contested Mount Fuji hill climb. The firm's 175cc YC1 model was especially successful, winning the 250cc class in 1956 despite giving away 75cc to rival manufacturers' models.

THE GENESIS OF THE TZ

In 1958 Yamaha produced the YD1, the company's first 250cc motorcycle and a machine that would come to be recognized as the father of all future Yamaha 2-strokes. Italian influenced

in its styling, it was very different in appearance from the firm's previous efforts but still peculiarly Japanese. By 1961 the Yamaha Motor Company employed more than 3,000 people.

But Japanese motorcycles lacked the handling capabilities of most European machines, and these shortcomings were most obvious in road racing. Way back in Chapter 6 Colin Seeley was throwing a lifeline to the ancient AJS and Matchless singles, by building a revolutionary frame from Reynolds 531 tubing that first appeared in early 1966 with a G50 motor. It was 4kg (9lb) lighter than the standard Matchless frame, and maintained the single's competitiveness until the Yamaha TZ came along. But Seeley wasn't a naïve old-school reactionary, because he spotted how competitive Yamaha's 2-stroke 250 and 350 twins would become before the TZ was launched in 1973. His 'Yamsel' – a Yamaha motor in a Seeley frame – gave notice of what was to come.

The unbelievable happened in the 1971 Junior TT when Agostini's MV Agusta broke down on the opening lap. The crowd actually cheered when it was announced that the Italian had stopped at Ramsey, knowing they might actually get a race worth the name. As, one by one, the favourites' motorcycles – all Yama-

Evolution of the Yamaha production racers from the YDS1R (front) to a later TZ behind. MIDNIGHT BIRD

Yamaha TZ350. NEOZOON

ha twins – fell or failed Yorkshireman Tony Jefferies (father of the late TT legend David) came home first with a Yamsel. John Cooper had been favourite to win the Junior the previous year on a Yamsel and Joey Dunlop would make his Senior TT debut on a Yamsel in 1976. It was proof that Yamaha were onto something and, when they revolutionized chassis design with the TZ350C, it would become clear that any aspiring racer needed to make his cheque payable to the Japanese giant.

The beginning of the 1970s was a quieter time for innovation in motorcycle racing. New regulations brought in between 1969 and 1971 limited Grand Prix bikes to a maximum of six gears and fewer cylinders: maximums of four in the 500cc class, two in the 250 and 350cc classes, and just one in the lower capacities. These changes killed the 4-stroke in the smaller classes and Honda withdrew from racing in advance of their execution. Yamaha scaled down its efforts, focusing a little more on making its racers easier to ride and a little less seizure-prone, and on its long-term ambitions in the Blue Riband class with the TZ500 and Giacomo Agostini.

1973 was the first year the big stars boycotted the Isle of Man TT, and the year the Yamaha TZ350 was launched. They could

have been made for each other, although the TT organizers had imagined the Formula 750 event would become the big crowd pleaser, even gifting it the Senior TT's traditional Friday spot as the last race of the week. As the 1960s had edged towards the new decade a raft of new races were added to try to shore up visitor numbers. By 1972 the list of races ran to a 750cc production, 500cc Production, 250cc Production, Sidecar 750cc, Sidecar 500cc, Lightweight TT (racing 250s), Ultra Lightweight (125s) and the Formula 750 – an international standard for modified production models. And, of course, these were added to the traditional Junior (350) and Senior (500) TTs.

Historically, the 350 Junior machines were allowed in 500cc Senior TT races to make up numbers, and because they were unlikely to win. An AJS 7R was 15 to 20mph (24–32km/h) down on a Matchless G50 or a Manx Norton. There were oversize engines (whether declared or not) as well as short-stroke specials that might have been less than 499cc but performed better. However, as long as the 350 and 500cc limits were adhered to then all was well. And everybody knew that the scrutineers only measured the capacity of the first three bikes home.

A 350 TO BEAT 500S

But when Yamaha introduced the TZ's predecessors – their 1963 TD1 series and, especially, its successor, the 1965 TR2B – the status quo evaporated. The TR2B was more than capable of outperforming any British single of whatever capacity in all respects except perhaps absolute top speed on Isle of Man gearing. Their only real downside was a fondness for plug fouling and seizure but then, in 1967, the much less troublesome TD1-C appeared. While the ideas were very much Walter Kaaden's, stolen by Ernst Degner, Yamaha had the money, materials and manpower to make them work even on a mass-produced racer.

Yamaha had looked to Germany for a starting point for 2-stroke multis and especially the Adler twin. They studied this motorcycle but were surprised at the lack of attention to making it easy to manufacture in quantity. This is an important distinction between Japanese and European art and design:

the Japanese find beauty in improvement, Europeans in originality. And anyway, Japanese engineers, starting from scratch after World War II, looked for designs that could be quickly, economically and reliably made in brand-new factories.

How good Yamaha's 2-stroke twins were was perhaps best illustrated when Phil Read won the 250 World Championship in 1971 on a very special – but originally bought off-the-shelf – Yamaha twin developed by Ferry Brouwer. That was the last time a privateer won a World Championship.

Yet these Yamaha twins were simple air-cooled engines. Each cylinder had a single exhaust port. A pair of transfer ports allowed fresh charge, compressed in the crankcase, to rush into the cylinders, then flow across the piston to the rear cylinder wall, up that wall and across the underside of the spark plug, and then down to the exhaust port. Preventing most of this fresh charge from disappearing out the exhaust port was the heart of Kaaden's vison for a modern 2-stroke – the expansion chamber. As the charge was ignited, the ex-

Agostini again in 2011 with a TZ on a Yamaha celebration lap at Creg Ny Baa. He won the 1974 350cc world championship aboard a Yamaha twin. IOMTT.COM/DAVE KNEEN/PACEMAKER PRESS

Charlie Williams is very much associated with Yamaha twins at the Isle of Man TT.

haust port sends powerful sound wave out and, as that wave expands in the wide part of the pipe, it sends back low pressure to empty the cylinder. Then, as the sound wave hits the narrowing part of the pipe, its echo arrives just as the exhaust port is closing to prevent the next charge of fuel and air to escape before ignition.

The upside of all of this is that, all things being equal (although they never are) a 2-stroke can make twice the power of a 4-stroke for a given capacity. There are two big downsides: 2-strokes get much hotter than 4-strokes; and where 4-strokes can use the non-power cycles and crankcases to lubricate an engine, a crankcase-compression 2-stroke cannot.

The original solution to the first problem was big, heavy, iron components. The solution to the second is to mix lubricating oil in with the fuel. This, however, means a 2-stroke is only getting an oil supply when the throttle is open, the further the better, which is why 2-strokes proved surprisingly reliable on the Isle of Man, and more prone to seizure at stop-and-go circuits.

That the TZ was on the way was hinted at in 1971 when air-cooled factory twins first appeared with four lugs welded on the front down-tubes, upon which a radiator could be

mounted as and when required. By the end of that year the first prototype water-cooled top end was ready for the 1972 season. These were used to great effect by favoured riders, none more effectively than Jarno Saarinen, who clinched the 250cc championship that year and finished a close second in the 350cc class behind Agostini and the MV Agusta.

THE TZ350A ARRIVES

By the end of 1972 the Yamaha factory was ready to start production of the water-cooled production race machine, the TZ350A. It was based loosely upon the R5 roadster, making it eligible for US competition, but there were some notable differences. The primary gears provided the drive for the water pump, and the barrels were one-piece, allowing the transfer ports to be larger than with separate cylinder castings.

The inclusion of water cooling and other slight improvements over the TZ350's air-cooled TR3 predecessors saw Yamaha's 350cc production racer become almost unbeatable in the hands of the right rider. The engine's only significant changes to the TR3 was the transfer ports being altered to improve scavenging, though port timing remained as for the older model. Claimed power was 60bhp at 9,500rpm, from a 64 x 54mm bore and stroke giving 347cc. Compression was 6.9:1. Primary drive was by gear to a 6-speed gearbox. The chassis was utterly conventional with a tubular steel frame, 18-inch wheels and a four-leading-shoe front brake.

So suddenly here was a 350 that could, and would, win the Senior. This upset to the status quo would have quickly resulted in a whole field of 2-strokes, and rendered the British singles obsolete overnight. So the ACU insisted all Senior entries 'must be over 350cc'. Of course it didn't take long before people such as Ted Broad repurposed the TZ with eccentric crankpins made up to marginally increase the stroke and give 352cc, but it at least gave the lovely old English singles a few years' grace.

And with water cooling introduced with the TZ350, Yamaha solved the other problem with 2-strokes. The 1973 Senior TT saw Mick Grant made all the early running on his 352cc Yamaha TZ '350', leading old campaigner, Australian Jack Findlay, who was the eventual winner with his Suzuki twin. On lap 3 Grant crashed on some oil going into Parliament Square at Ramsey, and his Yamaha was too badly damaged for him to continue. Findlay pulled away from Peter Williams in the latter stages of the race as William's Arter Matchless G50 struck problems, and had over a minute to spare at the finish, with Charlie Sanby third, riding another Suzuki twin.

A SURPRISE WIN FOR SUZUKI

But those big 2-stroke Suzuki T500 Titans (or Cobras, depending on the market) dated from a 1968 design aimed at providing a generously proportioned tourer with the emphasis on torque and a cosseting ride. The TZ was a production version of Yamaha's Grand Prix World Championship-winning bikes that brought Rod Gould and Jarno Saarinen 250cc crowns. Once Mick Grant had proved its worth, anyone who could stretch the TZ beyond the 350cc limit had racers beating a path to their door over the winter of 1973–74. Yamaha offered a revised TZ, the TZ350B, for 1974 but it was little changed over the original.

Grant's week of bad luck had started in the Junior TT, again leading on his Yamaha TZ350. His chances of a maiden TT victory were wrecked when he needed a 12-minute pit stop to replace a broken fairing bracket, and Tony Rutter took over to secure his maiden TT win, with Ken Huggett second and John Williams third. All were on Yamaha twins: indeed all bar six of the forty-four finishers were so equipped.

Another first-time TT winner that week was Charlie Williams, who became the latest of the new TT breed by winning the four-lap 250cc Lightweight TT after a tremendous battle with namesake – but not relative – John. At the finish Charlie held a 25-second advantage over John, with Bill Rae third. This time only three of thirty-six finishers were without a Yamaha twin. The message was clear: if you

Using the crankcase for compression means that 2-strokes burn off their oil supply to great effect.

wanted to be in with any sort of a chance in any race you needed to visit a Yamaha dealer.

Phil Carpenter used another TZ '350' to win the 1974 Senior TT, followed home by Charlie Williams and then Tony Rutter both again on the Yamaha twin. In fact, the top eight finishes were all mounted on similar bikes, as were twenty-four of the thirty-seven finishers. Rarely has a new model proved so immediately dominant.

HERETICS AT THE GATE

The purists would have pointed to Peter William's 105.47mph (169.70km/h) race average in the 1973 Formula 750 TT on a Norton twin as proof that this was the future of the TT. This was comfortably faster than Findlay and his Suzuki could manage in the Senior, but 1974 proved that the heretics were at the gate.

Bad weather decimated the 1974 programme but for many fans the Formula 750 TT was spoilt by the 352cc Yamaha twins proving more than a match for their big brothers. In a thrilling last lap Chas Mortimer saw off Charlie Williams's challenge by just 8.6 seconds with Tony Rutter third. All were on stretched TZ350s. In fairness the two Nortons 750s, ridden by Peter Williams and Dave Croxford, went out on the first lap with piston issues. Mick Grant, handicapped by an arm injury, found his 2-stroke, 3-cylinder, 750 Kawasaki too much of a handful, and Percy Tait could only finish fourth, behind the Yamahas, on his ex-works Triumph triple.

It was the same old story in the Senior TT, reduced to five laps because of the weather. Findlay and Paul Smart rode factory 2-stroke 4-cylinder Suzuki RG500s, but they were no match for the 352cc Yamaha twins in the treacherous conditions. The race had started in the dry with Williams' Yamaha taking the early lead, but as the rain fell he dropped back to let them get on with it. Eventually Phil Carpenter emerged as the surprise winner from Charlie Williams and Rutter.

Tony Rutter won his second Junior race in a row with another TZ, this time a sub-350cc machine. Early leader Charlie Williams retired on the third lap, and Mortimer also pulled out giving Rutter a comfortable run to the flag, with Grant

Chas Mortimer must be the man who enjoyed the greatest connection to Yamaha's racing 2-strokes. This is Jurby.

second and Paul Cott third. All were on Yamaha twins: in fact all but four of the fifty finishers were so mounted.

Anyone hoping for a challenge to the TZ in 1975 was probably disappointed. Only two of the thirty-eight finishers didn't have a TZ – an Aermacchi in thirty-fourth and a Honda in thirty-seventh place. The only upset for TZ fans in the Senior TT was Mick Grant's win with the Kawasaki triple; otherwise the TZ ruled both the Junior and Senior races.

The World Championship was exactly the same. If you exclude the Aermacchi Harley-Davidsons – which were in essence Yamaha twins with better chassis – everybody in the 250 and 350 class was on a Yamaha. It was almost the same in the 500 class, albeit often with the 4-cylinder straight four, basically doubling up the TZ250. Suzuki's new RG500 was starting to make waves, and the MV Agustas of Phil Read and Franco Bonera were still first and second in the championship, but Yamaha's 2-strokes had pretty much taken over. You could understand why the ACU had tried to keep them out, and why the FIM belatedly realized they should never have been allowed in. But Tony Rutter, something of a legend aboard a TZ250 or 350, admitted that they had anotaher downside:

They were fast, But they were so expensive to run. You had to keep replacing stuff, everything had a mileage limit and it was only ever a few hundred miles. Even the crankshaft was supposed to be changed after no more than 800 miles.

If a rider wanted to make his TZ pay as much start money as possible at the TT, it would run in both the Senior (with the longer stroke 352cc crank) and in the Junior TT with the standard crank and 347cc. Some very famous riders would have mystery problems on the final lap in the Junior, slowing or stopping altogether as they realized they were on for a top-three finish. The top three finishers always have their engines striped and measured by the scrutineers, and changing the crankshaft was a lot of work. Better to finish down the rankings than get disqualified and disgraced for having an illegal 352cc motor.

A SUSPENSION REVOLUTION

The TZ350C model of 1976 was hugely revised, a radical makeover given to the chassis and running gear wise from the earlier TZs. Adjustable and patented Monocross – monoshock rear suspension – was Yamaha's revolution, although they were almost beaten to it by Suzuki. The story started just five years earlier at a Belgium motocross meeting.

Chas Mortimer ready for the parade lap at the Classic TT.

One of the great supporters of Belgian motocross was Lucien Tilkiens, an engineer and manufacturer of industrial steam cleaning machines and water softeners. He also taught mechanical engineering at Liège University but was especially popular with motocross riders, always happy to help, even making special parts.

So when in 1971 Tilkiens' son, Guy, crashed heavily right in front of his dad there was a 'light bulb' moment. Tilkiens senior realized that the near-vertical rear shock absorbers had simply run out of travel and had nowhere to dissipate the energy of a heavy landing. Much better would be to lay the shocks down, pointing towards the steering head, to give as much travel as possible and allowing energy to be dissipated at one of the strongest parts of the frame. Of course there couldn't be two shock absorbers running either side of the bike, so he imagined one in the centre of the machine. This also meant that the swing arm could be braced to prevent

Yamaha RD400, successor to the RD350. Yamaha's advertising emphasized the 'race-developed' RD range, but in truth they shared less with the racers than many assumed.

twisting and that there was no need to make sure that two shock absorbers performed identically. And, just because he could, that's what he built for Guy's CZ single.

Guy liked the new chassis and throughout 1972 he and his father evolved the monoshock chassis, eventually asking Suzuki factory riders Roger DeCoster and Sylvain Geboers to try it out. They also liked it and suggested the Tilkiens build a version with a Suzuki motor that would allow direct comparison with the existing works bikes and an overture to Suzuki buying the rights. Before signing up, however, Suzuki wanted their own engineers to be certain that their riders' subjective opinions were backed up with good old theoretical engineering. It was a bad idea that would be compounded by some very bad luck.

Yamaha works rider Katsuhiko Sao and development engineer Toshinori Suzuki spotted Guy Tilkiens' Suzuki, apparently bereft of rear suspension. Suzuki – the irony of his name! – realized the worth of the idea and that he needed to act

quickly, given that this was an idea that Yamaha knew Suzuki were testing. Once Lucien Tilkiens had been identified as the designer and builder of the frame, three senior Yamaha officials flew from Japan to Belgium to see if Tilkiens would be open to offers for his idea.

Fortunately for Yamaha, Suzuki were now two months into assessing the monoshock but unable to believe there was any theoretical reason for the idea being sound. Yamaha, on the other hand, had been desperately searching for an alternative to the limits of current suspension designs. They signed a letter of agreement, but allowed Tilkiens a week's grace to go back to Suzuki. Suzuki still prevaricated, and when Honda came knocking on Tilkiens door he realized how big his idea was going to be. Honourably he gave Suzuki the week, and then sold up to Yamaha. Thirty patents later Yamaha had Monocross long-travel suspension on their works motocrossers and immediately every other bike in the sport was obsolete. The same would soon be true in road racing, and

The TZ twins helped development of the 500 fours such as this YZR500.

the TZ350C was the first chance for privateers to buy into a brave new world.

Combined with twin-piston front and rear disc brakes, the TZ350C was a worldwide sales hit. The UK retail price of around £1,500 included a comprehensive spares kit and represented incredible value for money. Like the Manx Norton all those years ago, here was a motorcycle a privateer might win a World Championship with. Almost insignificant was the small power increase to 62bhp at 10,000rpm.

YAMAHA TZ HEGEMONY

The 1976 Junior TT – the TT's final year as a World Championship round – saw Bill Smith's Suzuki coming home in 25th place the sole hiccough in Yamaha's hegemony. John Williams did a bit better in the Senior TT with a seventh for his Suzuki. The Senior TT top three was Tom Herron, Ian Richards and Billy Guthrie, all on TZs. In the Junior TT the win had gone to Chas Mortimer, chased home by Tony Rutter then Billy Guthrie. Ten minutes covered over twenty finishers in some two hours of racing in both events: before the TZ, typically

there would be more like half an hour between the winner crossing the line and the twenty-odd placings following them home. The TZ democratized racing and made it closer, if rather homogenous.

But the cream still rose to the top. Tom Herron would be runner-up in the 1977 350cc World Championship to Yamaha factory rider Takazumi Katayama. Charlie Williams finished in tenth place in the 1974 500cc World Championship and won the 1980 Formula II World Championship. Chas Mortimer had second and third places in the 125 World Championship and is the only rider to have won World Championship races on a 125, 250, 350, 500 and 750. Like the Manx Norton many seasons before, the sheer affordability and competiveness of the TZ range allowed a rider a shop window on the world stage. If you were good enough people would notice, knowing everybody was on the same bike.

The rightness of the Yamaha's design meant it would continue to dominate the 250 and 350 classes apart from the occasional upset, notably Kawasaki's intriguing longitudinal twin. But then Kawasaki seemed to pursue a strategy of doing things differently, although Yamaha, with their 2-stroke twins at least, found that evolution was what worked for them.

CHAPTER FOURTEEN

KAWASAKI HI/2R AND KR750

Businessman Shozo Kawasaki founded the Kawasaki Tsukiji Shipyard in Tokyo in 1878. Other yards soon followed, and in the early twentieth century Kawasaki Heavy Industries moved into the production of submarines, railway locomotives, steel bridges, trucks, buses, luxury cars and aircraft. In 1940 aircraft manufacture moved to Akashi, the current home of Kawasaki Motorcycles, where the firm built the Ki-61 Hien fighter plane.

Post-war, the company's aircraft division made gearboxes for motorcycle manufacturers and a high-quality 150cc 2-stroke engine. A 250cc 4-stroke 'KH' engine was manufactured in 1952. Other engines followed, both 2- and 4-stroke, and a scooter became the first two-wheeler to carry the Kawasaki name. In the late 1950s, as Honda, Suzuki and Yamaha

became stronger and other Japanese motorcycle manufacturers fell by the wayside, Kawasaki prepared to enter the market as a volume motorcycle manufacturer in its own right. In November 1960 the much respected and prestigious motorcycle company Meguro began to be absorbed by Kawasaki.

Meguro's skilful engineers were the arch copiers of the Japanese industry. The firm had moved on to successfully replicate many British designs over a great number of years, latterly BSA twins, and also the Harley-Davidson Type 97 V-twin. Despite lacking originality, Meguro motorcycles were well engineered and, in most respects, far better machines than the original motorcycles they so closely resembled.

In 1961 Kawasaki produced its first complete motorcycle, a 125cc 2-stroke called the Meihatsu B7, and a Tokyo office was

The 500cc Kawasaki H1 Mach III was the starting point for the racing H1R.

Like the H1R, the 750-class H2R was based on the road bike.

opened. But it was never Kawasaki's intention to challenge Honda's dominant market position, nor did the factory always consider it necessary to enter motorcycle races primarily to win. Motorcycle manufacture was not seen as one of the conglomerate's core businesses. For Kawasaki's motorcycle division, it was most of all important to be different, and to make people notice the Kawasaki brand.

As well as growing its gigantic steel-making operation throughout the 1960s and continuing to build ocean-going ships, aircraft and rolling stock, the Kawasaki group diversified into making industrial robots, and built industrial gas turbines and cement manufacturing equipment.

In 1963 Kawasaki's bikes started to be badged as such and included a new 125cc 2-stroke single, the B8. In 1966 Kawasaki produced the 650cc W1, a larger-capacity version of Meguro's earlier copy of BSA's A7 parallel twin. It was a well-engineered motorcycle, far superior to the original Small Heath machine, with a much stronger bottom end and oil tight casings.

The A1 Samurai and A7 Avenger 2-stroke twins, although rare in Britain, sold well in the USA. They were exciting, high-performance motorcycles. Kawasaki had found a direction and, in the stunningly fast 500cc triple, they found a way to be different quickly.

By 1968 the motorcycle market was shifting from utilitarian transport to more aggressive sporting motorcycles. The American market, especially, favoured quicker quarter-mile times (the time needed to accelerate from a standing start until a quarter of a mile had been covered), which were prominently advertised by manufacturers. While Kawasaki had a 750cc inline four 4-stroke in development, it was not going be ready in time to upstage the 1969 Honda CB750, so instead they moved up the release of their conventional piston port 2-stroke triple range. This was the N100 Plan, started in June 1967 with the intention of offering the motorcycle with the best power-to-weight ratio of any production model.

THE QUICKEST OF THE QUICK

The result of this was the H1/Mach III, with a 15-degree inclined inline 3-cylinder, 2-stroke motor first produced in September 1968. Compression was 6.8:1 with bore and stroke at 60 x 58.8mm, giving 498cc and 60bhp at 7,500rpm. Carburation was by three 28mm Mikunis. Weighing in at 188kg (414lb), the standing quarter mile was claimed at 12.4 seconds with a 124mph (199.52km/h) top speed. Although Honda's CB750 claimed another 7bhp it also weighed an extra 38kg (84lb) and so was over a second slower over the quarter mile than the Kawasaki. With its rapid acceleration and wayward handling, one magazine dubbed the H1 the world's fastest camel, but the new model sold well with total production eventually exceeding 110,000 motorcycles. Unsurprisingly Kawasaki introduced the Mach IV H2 in 1972, a 748cc (71 x 63mm) version with 74bhp that was even quicker, given it was barely any heavier than the 500.

Kawasaki introduced the first of their racing versions of the H1 with the 1970 H1R 500. The motor was based surprisingly closely on the H1 road bike, the most obvious differences being the dry clutch, larger (34mm or 35mm) carburettors, modified port timing, a higher compression ratio and

When Mick Grant brought his KR750 to the Isle of Man it was placed at the entrance to the VIP suite.

a close-ratio (but still 5-speed) gearbox. Naturally it was far lighter than the road bike on which it was based, but had an extra 15bhp.

A new twin-loop frame was used, together with a large Kawasaki front drum brake. The cross-over left-hand header pipe was unique to the H1R, important to keep all three expansion chambers' dimensions as close to one another as possible. Output was 75bhp at 9,000rpm with a dry weight of 130kg (287lb).

WORLD CHAMPIONSHIP SUCCESS – BUT NO TT ENTRY

Some thirty-five were built. New Zealander Ginger Molloy finished second to Agostini for the 1970 season with four second places, while long-time Kawasaki campaigner (and 1969 125cc Championship winner) Dave Simmonds gave the marque its first 500cc victory in the final race of the 1971 season, at the Spanish Grand Prix.

Ginger Malloy was actually at the Bultaco factory, his previous employer, when the call to race the Kawasaki came from America. It was a proposition he couldn't turn down from former Continental Circus racer Andy Richman, who was now with Bultaco's importer in his native United States.

Would Ginger race the 1970 Daytona 200 on a Kawasaki H1R? Andy could get the bike for a bargain $1,500, a promotion for the Daytona 200 only, but the bike had to leave the US after the race. 'Perfect for me!' Molloy recalls. So Andy ordered the H1R and arranged Ginger's travel details, covering expenses with his Cemoto East (Bultaco importers) Master

Charge credit card. 'Bultaco didn't know anything about it.' Malloy confided. 'I was sponsored by Bultaco in Europe, and unofficially also in America, on a Kawasaki.'

Ginger finished seventh in that star-studded 1970 Daytona 200, behind winner Dick Mann on the works Honda 750, Gene Romero, Don Castro and Yvon Duhamel. Keeping his end of the deal, Molloy took the Kawasaki back to Europe, campaigning it in the 1970 500cc World Championship. He finished second to a dominant Giacomo Agostini on the MV Agusta, and became an expert rebuilder of H1R crankshafts.

Ironically, the Senior TT was the only round of the championship Malloy didn't compete in although he finished every other round, which is how he beat Agostini's team-mate Angelo Bergamonti to second place in the title fight. But Bill Smith took an H1R to a podium finish in the 1970 Senior TT, admittedly several minutes behind winner Agostini (who won every round bar one of the year's 500cc World Championship) and Peter Williams' Arter Matchless.

The H1R and H2R factory and development rider was the French-Canadian Yvon Duhamel. Kawasaki had hired Duhamel in 1971, and he proved to be one of the few riders in the world who could tame the narrow power band and explosive power of the 2-stroke triple. He gave Kawasaki its first AMA national victory in September 1971 at Talladega, Alabama. From 1971 to 1973, Duhamel remained Kawasaki's most successful rider and lead development rider.

In 1971 Dave Simmonds rode an H1R to victory at the season-ending Spanish Grand Prix at Jarama, while Agostini sat out the race having already won the championship. It would mark Kawasaki's first victory in the premier 500cc class. Simmonds also finished second to Agostini at the Finnish Grand Prix and had third places at Assen and Monza, to secure

Mick Grant and Kawasaki KR750 in the 1976 Classic TT at Ballaugh Bridge. TTRACEPICS.COM

fourth place in the riders' championship. This placed Kawasaki third in the constructors' championship.

INTRODUCING KAWASAKI'S UK STAR – MICK GRANT

The following season, 1972, Kawasaki finished the constructors' championship in fourth place. The best results of the year were a second place in Spain for Simmonds and a third at the Isle of Man Senior TT for Mick Grant.

A young Mick Grant's Velocette had failed to finish the 1970 Senior TT when Bill Smith took an H1R to a podium place, but it would be the bright green Kawasaki triples that Grant would become associated with. Two years later he'd repeat Smith's performance with a third place in the 1972 Senior TT behind the two MVs. Although Grant was almost 10 minutes down on Agostini, the Italian's new team-mate Alberto Pagani finished barely a minute and a half ahead of Grant. A legendary TT partnership had been born, although Grant would choose to race a Yamaha for the following two year's TTs.

Nothing significant was achieved by the H1R in 1973 as

Kawasaki's engineers realized they were now uncompetitive with Yamaha's inline 4-cylinder, water-cooled 2-strokes and set about deciding on their next move. So for the 1974 season Kawasaki's racing department unveiled two new 500cc air-cooled triples designated H1RW (W standing for works, not water-cooled as is sometimes written: the 1974 works bikes were air-cooled). The bikes were based on the 750cc racing H2R, but with smaller-diameter frame tubes: 35mm on the 500 rather than the 37mm used on the 750. The specific front-brake calipers were forged into the lower fork leg. These H1R-Ws also had six gears rather than the privateers' five.

But 1974 saw the triple bedevilled by mechanical problems and crashes, so Kawasaki insisted on developing a new, water-cooled H1RW for 1975. They were raced in several Grand Prixs, principally by Christian Léon, during the 1975 season but proved to be underpowered and suffered from poor reliability; eventually this third bike was relegated to being raided for spares. The two built for Grant and his team-mate Barry Ditchburn were converted to right-hand-side gear-shifts, as was still the traditional racing arrangement in Europe. Power was claimed as 88bhp at 9,500rpm with a dry weight of 136kg (300lb)

Inevitably with the rise in prestigious races for production-based 750s there was an H2R, first raced in 1972, but it handled terribly in what was basically a scaled-up H1R frame. During the year various frame prototypes were tried before an all-new design was settled upon. Frame number 1 was used by Duhamel from late 1972 into 1974. The air-cooled H2R suffered from constricted port design and a wide motor that had to be fitted high in the frame to provide adequate ground clearance, due it being heavily based on the road going H2's motor.

THE ALL-NEW KR750

Formula 750 rules had required two hundred examples of the basic design to have been made available, but this was reduced to just twenty-five units for 1975. Kawasaki gave up on the H2RW and instead introduced the water-cooled KR750 in 1975. This was not, as some thought, a water-cooled H2RW: it was a new, from the ground up, racing engine, built with super-strong magnesium alloy sand-cast cases, with three cylinders in a single block, and power delivered via a 6-speed gearbox. The KR750 weighed just 130kg (287lb), but made around 120bhp.

1975 was to be Grant and Kawasaki's TT. After two years aboard a stretched TZ350, Grant had upgraded to the latest H1RW, a water-cooled version of the works H1RW that was also new for 1975. Only three were built and they were supplied to Grant and his team-mate Barry Ditchburn, who would become irrevocably linked to the green and white leathers of the team. The third went to Duhamel.

Grant won the postponed Senior on the H1R Kawasaki, having admitted that this meant a juggling act between revving the bike to 11,500rpm and breaking the crank or sticking to the 9,500 redline and not having enough power to win. Chas Mortimer, on a Yamaha like all the other top men, was the early leader but dropped back after an over-long pit stop, allowing John Williams into the lead with Grant second. Grant pushed the Kawasaki to the front on lap 5 and crossed the line with over half a minute to spare from Williams, with Mortimer having fought back to third. Ditchburn and the other H1RW came home twentieth in what would be his only TT.

The final race of the 1975 TT was the Classic, effectively a Formula 750 race with a field full of Yamaha TZ750s. Hailwood's lap record of 108.77mph (175.01km/h) had stood since 1967, and Grant smashed it convincingly as he powered his Kawasaki to a 109.82mph (176.70km/h) lap on his second tour of the course. In the excellent book *Chris Carter At Large*, the eponymous co-author remembers just how remarkable that was. He was signalling at Gooseneck for Grant and on hearing on Manx Radio that Grant had a 42-second lead, prepared to hold up a board with 'P1 +42' (position 1, 42-second lead) for the rider to see. To Carter's amazement Grant slowed as he approached, changing down the gearbox to come to a complete stop. Nodding at the board Grant called 'That's not bad is it?' before howling off up the mountain to set the new lap record.

Hailwood's lap record was set as he chased down Agostini, not realizing that the Italian was out of the race with a broken

The KR750 was built from the ground up as a pure-bred racer.

Compare this road bike-based **H2R** with the factory racer **KR750**.

Although Mick Grant is forever associated with Kawasaki triples, he also raced the RG500 and, famously, Honda's NR500.

chain. In an ironic twist, Grant's Reynolds' chain snapped on his next lap and Yamaha-mounted John Williams inherited the lead. After less than a lap Tony Rutter moved ahead, but his race ended on the fifth lap when the chain came off as his Yamaha jumped Ballaugh Bridge. Williams went on to secure a popular victory from Percy Tait and Charlie Sanby.

The H1RW was upgraded with a KR750-style front end in 1976, but to no avail. Grant failed to finish either the Senior or the Classic TTs and, realizing Yamaha and Suzuki had far bigger racing departments than Kawasaki, the H1R's days at the front were over. The KR750, especially, was campaigned in the UK for a few more years by Grant and Ditchburn. Although it was beyond the World Championship years, Grant had two KR750s in 1977 and 1978, which were nearly identical. In 1977 Grant managed a controversial 191mph (307.2km/h) at the TT and lapped at 112.77mph (181.45km/h). With the 1978 KR750 he won the 1978 Classic TT and raised the lap record to 114.33mph (183.96km/h). But the big Kawasaki triples sat in an increasingly difficult space next to the other Japanese factories' better-resourced efforts. The factory Yamahas and new Suzuki RG500 were simply better bikes, and Grant would moved on to the remarkable, if ill-starred, Honda NR500 project.

CHAPTER FIFTEEN

SUZUKI TR/RG500

The son of a cotton farmer, Michio Suzuki was born in 1887 in what was then the village of Hamamatsu. In 1909 he started a successful loom manufacturing business in the growing town. In 1937 the company imported an Austin 7 car and, by World War II, Suzuki had built several prototype automobiles, all powered by engines of the firm's own design.

During World War II Suzuki produced munitions, and afterwards resumed loom manufacture as well as taking on a variety of engineering and manufacturing contracts in order to survive. By this time Michio Suzuki's son-in-law Shumzo was taking a leading role in the firm's affairs and, as was Japanese tradition, had become his adopted son.

The TR500 may have been based on a road bike but it still won a Senior TT when it was a round of the 500cc world championship. BONHAMS

Paul Smart reminisces about his time racing TR and RG500 Suzukis.

In the early 1950s Suzuki designed its own 36cc 2-stroke engine, which it used in the manufacture of a powered bicycle called the Power Free. The Power Free soon became a two-speeder and the engine grew to 50cc. More models followed including the highly successful Diamond Free and, by 1954, Suzuki was making 4,000 Diamond Frees a month, now also exporting them to Taiwan. That year the Suzuki Motor Company was formed and Suzuki manufactured its first real motorcycle, the Colleda CO.

Colleda is Japanese for 'this is it'. 'It' was a 90.5cc 4-stroke motorcycle with a 3-speed gearbox, although the model was short-lived as Suzuki focused on improving its 2-stroke engines and producing the best electrical systems in the Japanese motorcycle industry.

In 1956 came a peculiar-looking 250cc 2-stroke twin, the SJK Colleda TT. It had a huge petrol tank and headlamp, Earles forks and an engine based – like the Yamaha twins – on a German Adler. A 125cc twin followed and the now globally familiar Suzuki 'S' logo first appeared in 1958. Suzuki's response to the Honda Super Cub was a 50cc 2-stroke commuter machine. Not a step-through as such, it had a small, low petrol tank mounted ahead of the rider.

The firm opened a London office in 1961, following its first TT entry the previous year. Also in 1961, Suzuki was party to the defection of East German MZ racer Ernst Degner, who was a skilled mechanic as well as a rider. Degner brought with him many 2-stroke design and tuning secrets learned from his employers DKW (parent to the MZ team), and from his mentor, the highly gifted engineer Walter Kaaden.

Suzuki won the 50cc world road racing championship the following year and other successes followed. Race director Masanao Shimizu was later put in charge of the Suzuki road bike programme, and the scintillating 250cc Super Six (as in six gears, then unheard of on a road bike) appeared in Britain in 1967. By 1970 it had become the Hustler and was being sold alongside the T500.

Suzuki's 500cc parallel twin 2-stroke remained in production for almost a decade from 1967, with over 100,000 examples built. Known initially as the Cobra, and then as the Titan and GT500, the T500 proved to be a reliable, practical

2-stroke that offered a Triumph Bonneville-matching 46bhp in the compact dimensions of a middleweight even if it actually weighed more than a Bonneville.

The 492cc air-cooled engine adopted the layout of Suzuki's smaller twins although it was very oversquare with a 70 x 64mm bore and stroke. Despite this, the power delivery was almost lazy by 2-stroke standards.

A 5-speed gearbox was all it needed, although Suzuki made a few modifications to the frame to address criticism of its handling. These came into much greater focus when the T500 was raced, especially in France, because the racing version, the TR500, was initially developed in Boulogne. Pierre Bonnet was the French Suzuki importer and the works team was based with him for their first serious attempt at the World Championships in 1962. With Ernst Degner they won the 50cc championship first time out, the East German also taking 11th in the 125 championship. His team-mate, New Zealander Hugh Anderson, finished 7th.

By 1967 Jacques Roca, a talented Spanish-French racer and engineer had joined forces with Bonnet. Shortly after the T500 roadster was launched, Roca built and raced a racing version that so impressed Suzuki that the factory, although officially retired from World Championship racing, decided

Without the fairing it is clear that this is the later water-cooled version of the TR500. BONHAMS

to offer a production version. A suitably tweaked version of the T500 motor was fitted into an all-new Norton Featherbed-inspired frame with Ceriani 230mm twin leading-shoe front brake and Ceriani forks, designated the XR05 or TR500. It offered 63.5bhp at 8,000rpm and weighed 135kg (298lb). Ron Grant ran to fifth at the 1968 Daytona 500 on the TR500 and Mitsuo Itoh managed ninth.

By the early 1970s the TR500 was making over 70bhp and for 1973 water cooling was added, taking the weight to 140kg (307lb). A new frame was introduced, which was further updated with twin front disc brakes and a single disc at the rear. This was the model Jack Findlay used to win the 1973 the Isle of Man Senior TT.

This was the first year the TT was boycotted by the factories and star riders although, of course, it remained a round of the World Championship. Spectators and organizers alike were nervously asking themselves if the TT could survive without them. Certainly the 1973 races proved that they could as a fresh wave of TT riders hit the headlines, hopeful of glory and catching the eye of a sponsor with none of the big names to compete with. However, it wasn't a new star but rather an old campaigner, Australian Jack Findlay, who was the popular winner of the Senior, riding the Suzuki twin.

Mick Grant had made all the early running on his 352cc Yamaha, leading Findlay and Peter Williams's Arter Matchless. On lap 3 Grant crashed on some oil going into Parliament Square and his Yamaha was too badly damaged for him to continue. Findlay pulled away from Williams in the latter stages as the Matchless single struck problems, and had over a minute to spare at the finish. Charlie Sanby was third, on an ex-Barry Sheene-Seeley framed water-cooled TR500.

That the TR500 motor, especially in water-cooled form, was competitive is proven by not only Colin Seeley building a version but also by being used in one of the very first Bimotas, the 1975 SB1. But, as we've seen, this was really a footnote in the story of the Yamaha TZ350's dominance. The T500, even with water cooling, was no match for the long-stroke 352cc Yamaha, especially when the TZ was updated with Monocross suspension for 1976. The TR500 was still in essence a road bike developed by the French importer and then put into small-scale production. The Yamaha TZs were off-the-shelf Grand Prix racers. Suzuki, flushed with the success of the last few years in 500cc racing, accepted that they needed to invest substantially in a new bike if they were to continue winning world-class 500cc races.

The paddocks of the Continental circus and the Isle of Man TT were packed with a selection of rider-owned and prepared motorcycles: Italian twins, British singles, and the nas-

cent Japanese 2-strokes, headed by the stretched 350 Yamahas and the first-generation air-cooled privateer 500s, such as the TR500 Suzuki twins and Kawasaki H1R triples. But this transitional group was easy prey for the factory 4-cylinder 500s of MV Agusta and Yamaha.

Unsurprisingly Yamaha were the first to build a 2-stroke 500cc four with the 1973 0W20 or YZR500. Looking to all the world like a pair of TZ250s bound together to give a transverse 4-cylinder motor, the works racer was victorious in the first two rounds of the 1973 season, ridden by Jarno Saarinen. Phil Read and MV won the next round and then, at Monza, Saarinen was killed. It would be 1975 before the big Yamaha claimed the championship with Agostini.

But Yamaha never intended to let mere mortals ride their bikes while Suzuki, as with the TR500, intended to build a bike they could sell to privateers. After all, as Yamaha had proven with their twins, you can advertise your engineering genius to fans while actually turning a profit.

SUZUKI'S HISTORY OF SQUARE FOUR MOTORS

The disadvantage of a straight 4-cylinder motor is width (or length, depending on how it is installed) but, as with the original Italian designs, it helps cooling. However once water cooling is adopted this ceases to be much of an issue, and Suzuki reasoned that a square four (basically two parallel twins, one behind the other) crammed as much power into as small a space as possible.

This wasn't a new idea at Suzuki. Their 1965 RS6 prototype was a 124.7cc square four with disc inlet valves and water cooling. Although it gave 34bhp, compared with Suzuki's existing twin's 30bhp, this was at 16,000rpm rather than 13,000rpm and even eight gears were nothing like enough. Two years earlier Suzuki had raced a 247.3cc square four with a very similar layout, with two of their 125 parallel twins bolted together. It proved problematic and probably cost Suzuki World Championships in the smaller classes as their engineers battled to make it work, let alone win. Yet over a decade later metallurgy was much improved, as were Suzuki's resources and expertise. It was time to revisit the lessons of the past.

So after six years away from full-time World Championship racing, Suzuki's tacit support of Jack Findlay during 1973 with the TR500 convinced them that they were ready to take on the MV Agusta Quattro and Yamaha's YZR500. The Hamam-

Designer Massimo Tamburini was so taken with the XR14's underseat exhausts that he vowed to fit them to a road bike. He finally succeeded with the Ducati 916. DAMO 1977

Wil Hartog was closely linked to the RG500 – and white leathers. NETHERLANDS NATIONAL ARCHIVE

atsu firm's challenger for the Blue Riband class was an all-new square-four 2-stroke, the XR14 RG500. Like its 125 and 250cc predecessors the RG500 had disc-valve induction and twin geared-together crankshafts, this time limited by the FIM rule to driving a 6-speed gearbox via an intermediate gear. Unlike its predecessors, the RG's cylinders were separate so that a problem on one did not require the other cylinders to be disturbed. Each cylinder had five transfer ports with a bore and stroke of 56 x 50.5mm to give a 497.5cc. Four Mikuni VM34 (mm) SS carburettors sat either side of the crankcases. Compression was 8:1 and the clutch was a dry multiplate. It weighed 135kg (298lb) and initially maximum output was 90bhp at 10,500rpm, quickly raised to 100bhp at 11,200rpm. This state-of-the-art power unit was housed in a conventional tubular-steel twin-loop frame. Kayaba suspension was conventional front and rear with floating front 270mm twin discs. The rear 250mm disc was ventilated.

Early teething issues included the inevitable seizures as Suzuki searched for the ideal fuelling. It was also prone to bad primary drive gearbox breakages, rather terrifying for the rider. Even so, Findlay's fifth in the 1974 500cc World Championship was probably the best that could be hoped for. Phil Read won followed by MV Agusta team-mate Franco Bonera. Behind them were the factory Yamahas of Teuvo Lansivuori and Agostini.

For the 1974 TT the Formula 750 race was billed as the top attraction, replacing the Senior as the final race of the week. But foul weather wreaked havoc with the programme, including in the Senior TT, which was reduced to five laps because of the conditions. Findlay and Paul Smart rode prototype 4-cylinder Suzuki RG500s, but they were no match for the 352cc Yamaha twins in the slippery conditions. The race started in the dry and Williams took on the Yamahas, but as the rain fell he dropped back and let them get on with it. Eventually Phil Carpenter emerged as the surprise winner from Charlie Williams and Rutter. The top eight finishers were on Yamaha twins, ninth and tenth being taken by Matchless singles, indicative of just how difficult conditions were. And this was the fifth round of the World Championship.

Despite his past efforts and loyalty Findlay was sacked at the end of 1974. Suzuki passed the management of the team to British Heron corporation under the Suzuki GB (Great Britain) banner. The rider line-up was impressive, including the young and upcoming star Barry Sheene, the darling of the press. Finn Teuvo Länsivuori and Brit John Newbold completed the international competitors with Stan Woods also entered in UK races.

Inevitably Agostini ran away with the 1975 title chase at the start of the season, with Mick Grant and Kawasaki winning the Senior TT, the largely boycotted round six of the championship. Of course, now as the official Suzuki Grand Prix team, the Suzuki GB team stayed away from the Isle of Man and not a single RG500 competed. The next championship round was Assen which Sheene won, taking the first 500cc World Championship win for both him and the RG500. It was also Suzuki's first win in the premier 500cc class if – as many often seem to – you exclude Findlay's Senior TT win in 1973.

AN OVER-THE-COUNTER WORLD CHAMPIONSHIP WINNER

Before the first twenty-five Mark 1 RG500s went on sale ready for the 1976 season it had become inconceivable that a privateer might run at the front of the Blue Riband class. It's become a cliché to call the Suzuki the Manx Norton of the 2-stroke Grand Prix age, but it truly was. For over a decade, from 1976 to 1986, the square four evolved and continued to fill grids around the world, to the delight of organizers and fans. It really is impossible to over-emphasize the effect the RG500 had when it first went on sale, as the results of the 1976 World Championship illustrate. With fifty-eight bikes delivered to eager buyers, no fewer than the first twelve riders in the final 500cc World Championship results were Suzuki-mounted, including household names such as Agostini, Read and Lucchinelli. It would remain a competitive privateer option right up until the end of the production run in 1990, winning Suzuki seven consecutive 500cc World Championship constructors' titles from 1976 to 1982. These included four World Championship riders' titles: in 1976 and 1977 for Barry Sheene; again for Marco Lucchinelli in 1981; and then Franco Uncini in 1982.

So 1976 was the final year that the Isle of Man TT was a round of the World Championship. The RG500 had been much improved over the winter, in terms of both reliability and power, now up to 114bhp at 11,000rpm. John Williams upped the lap record by nearly 3mph in a dramatic Senior TT, riding an RG500, leading Tom Herron and his Yamaha by almost three minutes going into the last lap and looking like the winner elect before slowing dramatically. He was indicated on the scoreboard at Signpost Corner, but then appeared pushing the big Suzuki from Governor's Bridge, having run out of petrol.

Inevitably Barry Sheene is the name most associated with the RG500. These are a few of his at the Goodwood Festival of Speed. BIG-ASHBEX

The great Barry Sheene.
REX/SHUTTERSTOCK

An early XR14 RG500 at Goodwood Festival of Speed. DAMO 1977

John Williams broke the lap record on an RG500 in the 1976 Senior TT, but ran out of fuel while leading and had to push home. TTRACEPICS.COM

Another view of the all-conquering 1976 Suzuki RG500 XR14. SILODROME.COM

With the crowd urging him on, he pushed over the line, collapsing with exhaustion and frustration. Herron was the winner from Ian Richards, with Billy Guthrie third. Williams was eventually able to claim seventh place. His consolation was a new lap record of 112.27mph (180.64km/h), but later in the week he was the comfortable winner of the Classic, which had been postponed by a day. He led aboard the RG500 from start to finish comfortably, leading the podium Yamahas of Alex George and Tony Rutter.

The RG500 won every round of the 1976 World Championship, a remarkable achievement especially given that some of them were over the counter privateer models. Phil Read has told the author that it was the finest motorcycle he ever raced, as has Tony Rutter. But Rutter also wistfully added that it brought the end of an era:

They were fast, and the RG500 was a wonderful bike, best bike I ever raced. But they were so expensive to run. You had to keep replacing stuff, everything had a mileage limit and it was only ever a few hundred miles. So you had to find the money and that meant everybody needed a sponsor, and there's only so many of them to go round.

So the motorcycle that gave privateers the last chance in history to win in the 500cc World Championship class also in effect brought to an end the age of the true privateer. The faster the RG became, the more expensive running one became. Sponsors appeared but they expected something in return. Guest appearances, smarter attire (Rutter was infamously denied access to an FIM championship ceremony for having no suit and tie) and most of all the need to read from a script. Initially superstars like Sheene could break the rules, but eventually everybody had to toe the line. Even Valentino Rossi, who for much of his career refused to ride with tobacco sponsorship, eventually had little choice but to do so.

So as the age of the TT as a World Championship round closed, so did the age of the true privateer. The Suzuki RG500 gave a privateer an opportunity that had not existed since the Manx Norton had been competitive on the world stage, while also closing the door on an era when it was possible to compete without serious levels of sponsorship.

CHAPTER SIXTEEN

EPILOGUE

While 1976 was the final Isle of Man TT that held the British rounds of the classic World Championship, there was a sop from the FIM. While the Isle of Man no longer hosted the 250cc, 350cc and 500cc classes (there were also 50cc and 125cc races in other rounds) 1977 saw the inauguration of the Formula TT World Championships. These awarded a World Championship to a rider and manufacturer for a single race, seemingly overgenerous but seen as necessary if the TT wasn't to fail within a few years. And, as they were based upon a single race rather than a series, there could be no compunction to compete if a team didn't want to race on the Isle of Man.

The Formula TT rules allowed a greater degree of engine tuning than the old production TT rules, as well as complete freedom of chassis design – aimed, the cynics decided, at allowing the Japanese factories' production models to be competitive on a course where their powerful but ill-handling superbikes had yet to prove themselves.

The categories were initially Formula 1, 2 and 3. Formula 1 ran 4-strokes of 600–1,000cc capacity against 2-strokes of 350–500cc. Formula 2 was for 4-strokes from 400–600cc and 2-strokes of 250–350cc. Finally, Formula 3 allowed racing between 4-strokes from 200–400cc against 2-strokes of 125–250cc. A win in 1977 would make the team and rider

Mike Hailwood about to overtake Phil Read on the road at Hairpin in the 1978 Formula I TT. RAY STEVENS

Dean Harrison heels the big BSA 750 triple in as he climbs the mountain.
IOMTT.COM/DAVE KNEEN/PACE-MAKER PRESS

FIM World Champions, a simple gimmick that many TT fans felt was scant recompense for moving the British Grand Prix from the Isle of Man to Silverstone in central England. The FIM probably thought the World Championship status for Formula racing mattered little, since most observers felt that losing Grand Prix status would mean that the TT would wither and die. How wrong they were.

In 1978 the Island's favourite adopted son Mike Hailwood returned to win aboard a big Ducati. Yet having decided to return to race at the Isle of Man TT, and having decided after racing Ducatis in Australia that he would like to run one of the big twins at the TT, it wasn't just Ducati that Mike approached. He and his manager Ted Macaulay's most obvious port of call was his old World Championship team, Honda. Ted was then a sports reporter the *Daily Mirror*, and recorded the story of Mike's return to the TT in the 1980 book, *Mike the Bike – again*. This includes the story of the Yamaha 2-stokes Hailwood rode in other 1978 TT races with big-money sponsorship from vermouth vendors Martini. But it is clear that Mike's affection was for the big Ducati, and that was where the chance of a win seemed greatest. Legendary mechanic Nobby Clark, however, felt the Yamahas would be unbeatable, although Mike failed to gel with the 750cc OW31.

Yet in the ostensibly production-based Formula 1 there was no obvious Yamaha road bike suitable for the race. So it was Honda or Ducati. Although some claim that Ted and Mike never approached Honda, there is actually clear photographic evidence of Mike, Ted and Gerald Davison of Honda UK in deep conversation at the 1977 Earl's Court show. Given that Gerald joined Honda just after Mike left them, they could hardly have been chatting about the good old days.

Perhaps half expecting to be rebuffed by Honda – Yamaha took some time to decide to support Hailwood, after all – Ted Macauley had already been in touch with Sports Motorcycles in late August 1977, having met Mike and Steve Wynne at the British Grand Prix at Silverstone a few weeks earlier. Ted lived only a few miles from Steve's Manchester premises and, like most, had felt that if the 1977 Formula 1 race hadn't been shortened from five to four laps Sports Motorcycles would have beaten the works Honda team. Steve secured a brace of hand-built 900F1s – emphatically not a 900SS-based bike, as is too often claimed – direct from Ducati.

Mike Hailwood's return brought record crowds to the Island and there was a party atmosphere as it became clear that he would win the TT Formula 1 race on the booming Ducati. Few believed he could do it but he led from the end of his fastest-ever TT lap: 109.87mph (176.78km/h). As he slowly closed on his old rival Phil Read on the roads the crowd cheered ever louder, becoming ecstatic when Mike passed the Honda Britain rider on the road. Trying to press the Ducati into a breakdown, it was actually Read who retired with a leaking oil cooler on the fifth lap at the eleventh Milestone.

As Mike crossed the line his Ducati also failed but it didn't matter. More than one person, including Mike, wiped away a few tears. It was one of those special moments that only witnessing a truly great sportsman in action can provide.

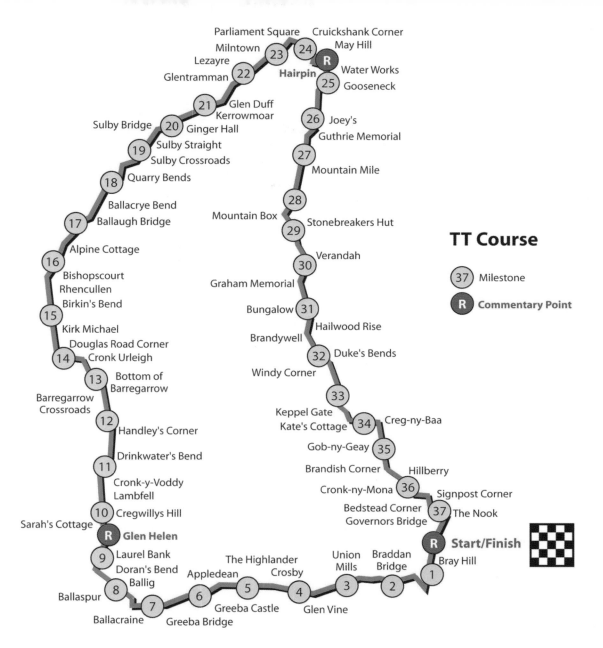

Parliament Square Cruickshank Corner
Milntown   May Hill
Lezayre   (23) (24)
Glentramman (22)   **R** Water Works
                      Hairpin (25)
          (21) Glen Duff   Gooseneck
Sulby Bridge   Kerrowmoar (26) Joey's
          (20) Ginger Hall   Guthrie Memorial
        (19) Sulby Straight (27)
              Sulby Crossroads   Mountain Mile
          (18) Quarry Bends (28)
                Ballacrye Bend   Mountain Box Stonebreakers Hut
          (17) Ballaugh Bridge (29)
              Alpine Cottage   Verandah
          (16)   (30)
              Bishopscourt   Graham Memorial
              Rhencullen
              Birkin's Bend   Bungalow (31)
          (15)   Hailwood Rise
              Kirk Michael   Brandywell
              Douglas Road Corner   (32) Duke's Bends
          (14) Cronk Urleigh   Windy Corner
        (13) Bottom of   (33)
              Barregarrow
Barregarrow   Keppel Gate (34) Creg-ny-Baa
Crossroads   Kate's Cottage
          (12)   Gob-ny-Geay (35)
              Handley's Corner   Brandish Corner   Hillberry
          (11) Drinkwater's Bend Cronk-ny-Mona (36)
              Cronk-y-Voddy   Signpost Corner
              Lambfell   Bedstead Corner (37) The Nook
          (10) Cregwillys Hill   Governors Bridge
Sarah's Cottage   **R** **Start/Finish**
        R **Glen Helen**   Bray Hill
        (9) Laurel Bank   The Highlander Union Braddan (1)
            Doran's Bend   Crosby   Mills Bridge
            Ballig Appledean   (2)
        (8)   (3)
Ballaspur   (5) (4)
        (7) (6)   Greeba Castle   Glen Vine
Ballacraine   Greeba Bridge

TT Course

(37) Milestone

R Commentary Point

Course map.

Unfortunately Mike's three other races on the Martini Yamahas that should have made him unbeatable were not so successful. In the Senior TT his steering damper broke at Ramsey and he crawled home in twenty-eighth place. Mike retired on the first lap of the Classic TT with engine trouble, and problems in the 250 Lightweight TT saw him limp home in twelfth.

And yet his job was done. Fans accepted the TT as a one-off special event, which is what it remains today. It has created heroes who can stand apart from the World Championship riders as legends in their own right such as John McGuiness and Guy Martin – indeed, Guy Martin is probably as famous as

MotoGP's Valentino Rossi. So while it was fantastic to see the TT as the British round of the classic World Championships for the twenty-seven years from 1949 until 1976, it is equally fantastic to see it today. Indeed access to the track, machinery and stars is far greater than at any MotoGP event because the aim of the Isle of Man TT is to draw people to the island. MotoGP is far more interested in television rights. It's hard to imagine how watching something from a distance on a screen can ever compare to watching people racing motorcycles on roads anybody can ride on up close and personal – which is what the TT remains.

TT PODIUM PLACINGS 1949–1976

Podium placings for the Senior and Junior TTs 1949–76 when they were the British rounds of the 500 and 350cc World Championships, respectively. The race times are in the format hours.minutes.seconds.tenths of a second. The average race speed is in miles per hour as recorded by the race officials.

1949 Senior TT

1	Harold L Daniell	Norton	3.02.18.6	86.93
2	Johnny Lockett	Norton	3.03.52.4	86.19
3	Ernie Lyons	Velocette	3.05.22.0	85.50

1949 Junior TT

1	Freddie L Frith	Velocette	3.10.26.0	83.15
2	Ernie Lyons	Velocette	3.11.08.0	82.92
3	Artie Bell	Norton	3.11.49.0	82.62

1950 Senior TT

1	Geoff Duke	Norton	2.51.45.6	92.37
2	Artie Bell	Norton	2.54.25.6	90.86
3	Johnny Lockett	Norton	2.55.22.4	90.37

1950 Junior TT

1	Artie Bell	Norton	3.03.35.0	86.33
2	Geoff Duke	Norton	3.04.52.0	85.73
3	Harold L Daniell	Norton	3.07.56.0	84.33

1951 Senior TT

1	Geoff Duke	Norton	2.48.56.8	93.83
2	Bill Doran	AJS	2:53.19.2	91.44
3	Cromie McCandless	Norton	2:55.27.0	90.33

1951 Junior TT

1	Geoff Duke	Norton	2.56.17.6	89.90
2	Johnny Lockett	Norton	2:59.35.0	88.25
3	Jack Brett	Norton	3:00.22.4	87.87

1952 Senior TT

1	HR [Reg] Armstrong	Norton	2.50.28.4	92.97
2	R Les Graham	MV Agusta	2.50.55.0	92.72
3	Ray Amm	Norton	2.51.31.2	92.40

1952 Junior TT

1	Geoff Duke	Norton	2.55.30.6	90.29
2	HR [Reg] Armstrong	Norton	2.56.57.8	89.55
3	Rod Coleman	AJS	2.58.12.4	88.93

1953 Senior TT

1	Ray Amm	Norton	2.48.51.8	93.85
2	Jack Brett	Norton	2:49.03.8	93.74
3	HR [Reg] Armstrong	Gilera	2:49.16.8	93.62

1953 Junior TT

1	Ray Amm	Norton	2:55.05.0	90.52
2	Ken T Kavanagh	Norton	2:55.14.6	90.44
3	Fergus Anderson	Moto Guzzi	2:57.40.6	89.41

1954 Senior TT

1	Ray Amm	Norton	1.42.46.8	88.12
2	Geoff Duke	Gilera	1:43.52.6	87.19
3	Jack Brett	Norton	1:45.15.2	86.04

1954 Junior TT

1	Rod Coleman	AJS	2.03.41.8	91.51
2	Derek Farrant	AJS	2:05.34.0	90.15
3	Bob Keeler	Norton	2:05.43.6	90.03

1955 Senior TT

1	Geoff Duke	Gilera	2.41.49.8	97.93
2	HR [Reg] Armstrong	Gilera	2.43.49.0	96.74
3	Ken T Kavanagh	Moto Guzzi	2.46.32.8	95.16

1955 Junior TT

1	Bill Lomas	Moto Guzzi	2.51.38.2	92.33
2	Bob McIntyre	Norton	2.52.38.2	91.79
3	Cecil Sandford	Moto Guzzi	2.53.02.2	91.59

1956 Senior TT

1	John Surtees	MV Agusta	2.44.05.8	96.57
2	John Hartle	Norton	2.45.36.6	95.69
3	Jack Brett	Norton	2.46.54.2	94.96

1956 Junior TT

1	Ken T Kavanagh	Moto Guzzi	2.57.29.4	89.29
2	Derek Ennett	AJS	3.02.07.4	87.02
3	John Hartle	Norton	3.04.48.6	85.75

1957 Senior TT

1	Bob McIntyre	Gilera	3.02.57.0	98.99
2	John Surtees	MV Agusta	3.05.04.2	97.86
3	Bob Brown	Gilera	3.09.02.0	95.81

1957 Junior TT

1	Bob McIntyre	Gilera	2.46.50.2	94.99
2	Keith Campbell	Moto Guzzi	2.50.29.8	92.95
3	Bob Brown	Gilera	2.51.38.2	92.34

1958 Senior TT

1	John Surtees	MV Agusta	2.40.39.8	98.63
2	R H F [Bob] Anderson	Norton	2:46.06.0	95.4
3	Bob Brown	Norton	2:46.22.2	95.25

1958 Junior TT

1	John Surtees	MV Agusta	2.48.38.4	93.97
2	Dave Chadwick	Norton	2.52.50.6	91.68
3	Geoff Tanner	Norton	2.53.06.4	91.54

1959 Senior TT

1	John Surtees	MV Agusta	3.00.13.4	87.94
2	Alistair King	Norton	3.05.21.0	85.5
3	Bob Brown	Norton	3.10.56.4	83

1959 Junior TT

I	John Surtees	MV Agusta	2.46.08.0	95.38
2	John Hartle	MV Agusta	2.49.12.2	93.65
3	Alistair King	Norton	2.49.22.6	93.56

1960 Senior TT

I	John Surtees	MV Agusta	2.12.35.2	102.44
2	John Hartle	MV Agusta	2.15.14.2	100.44
3	Mike Hailwood	Norton	2.18.11.6	98.29

1960 Junior TT

I	John Hartle	MV Agusta	2.20.28.8	96.7
2	John Surtees	MV Agusta	2.22.24.2	95.39
3	Bob McIntyre	AJS	2.22.50.4	95.11

1961 Senior TT

I	Mike Hailwood	Norton	2.15.02.0	100.61
2	Bob McIntyre	Norton	2.16.56.4	99.2
3	Tom Phillis	Norton	2.17.31.2	98.78

1961 Junior TT

I	Phil Read	Norton	2.22.50.0	95.11
2	Gary Hocking	MV Agusta	2.24.07.8	94.25
3	Ralph Rensen	Norton	2.25.03.0	93.65

1962 Senior TT

I	Gary Hocking	MV Agusta	2.11.13.4	103.51
2	Ellis Boyce	Norton	2.21.06.2	96.27
3	Fred J Stevens	Norton	2.21.09.4	96.24

1962 Junior TT

I	Mike Hailwood	MV Agusta	2.16.24.2	99.59
2	Gary Hocking	MV Agusta	2.16.29.8	99.52
3	Frantisek Šastný	Jawa CZ	2.23.23.4	94.74

1963 Senior TT

I	Mike Hailwood	MV Agusta	2:09.48.4	104.64
2	John Hartle	Gilera	2.11.01.8	103.67
3	Phil Read	Gilera	2.15.42.2	100.1

1963 Junior TT

I	Jim Redman	Honda	2.23.08.2	94.91
2	John Hartle	Gilera	2.29.58.2	90.58
3	Frantisek Šastný	Jawa CZ	2.31.20.6	89.76

1964 Senior TT

I	Mike Hailwood	MV Agusta	2.14.33.8	100.95
2	Derek Minter	Norton	2.17.56.6	98.47
3	Fred J Stevens	Matchless	2.20.54.6	96.4

1964 Junior TT

I	Jim Redman	Honda	2.17.55.4	98.51
2	Phil Read	AJS	2.25.00.6	93.58
3	Mike Duff	AJS	2.25.21.4	93.46

1965 Senior TT

I	Mike Hailwood	MV Agusta	2.28.09.0	91.69
2	Joe Dunphy	Norton	2.30.28.8	90.28
3	Mike Duff	Matchless	2.34.12.0	88.09

1965 Junior TT

1	Jim Redman	Honda	2:14.52.2	100.72
2	Phil Read	Yamaha	2.16.44.4	99.35
3	Giacomo Agostini	MV Agusta	2.17.53.4	98.52

1966 Senior TT

1	Mike Hailwood	Honda	2.11.44.8	103.11
2	Giacomo Agostini	MV Agusta	2.14.22.6	101.09
3	Chris Conn	Norton	2.22.26.8	95.37

1966 Junior TT

1	Giacomo Agostini	MV Agusta	2.14.40.4	100.87
2	Peter Williams	AJS	2.24.46.6	93.83
3	Chris Conn	Norton	2.26.45.4	92.56

1967 Senior TT

1	Mike Hailwood	Honda	2.08.36.2	105.62
2	Peter Williams	Matchless	2.16.20.0	99.64
3	Steve Spencer	Norton	2.17.47.2	98.59

1967 Junior TT

1	Mike Hailwood	Honda	2.09.45.6	104.68
2	Giacomo Agostini	MV Agusta	2.12.48.8	102.28
3	Derek Woodman	MZ	2.20.53.6	96.41

1968 Senior TT

1	Giacomo Agostini	MV Agusta	2.13.39.4	101.63
2	Brian Ball	Seeley	2.22.08.4	95.57
3	Barry Randle	Norton	2.22.08.8	95.56

1968 Junior TT

1	Giacomo Agostini	MV Agusta	2.09.38.6	104.78
2	Renzo Pasolini	Benelli	2.12.19.6	102.65
3	W A [Bill] Smith	Honda	2.22.58.6	95.02

1969 Senior TT

1	Giacomo Agostini	MV Agusta	2.09.40.2	104.75
2	Alan Barnett	Metisse	2.18.12.6	98.28
3	Tom Dickie	Seeley	2.18.44.2	97.92

1969 Junior TT

1	Giacomo Agostini	MV Agusta	2.13.25.4	101.81
2	Brian Steenson	Aermacchi	2.23.36.4	94.6
3	Jack Findlay	Aermacchi	2.24.41.2	93.89

1970 Senior TT

1	Giacomo Agostini	MV Agusta	2.13.47.6	101.52
2	Peter Williams	Matchless	2.18.57.0	97.76
3	W A [Bill] Smith	Kawasaki	2.21.07.6	96.26

1970 Junior TT

1	Giacomo Agostini	MV Agusta	2.13.28.6	101.77
2	Alan Barnett	Aermacchi	2.18.23.8	98.16
3	Paul A Smart	Yamaha	2.20.08.8	96.93

1971 Senior TT

1	Giacomo Agostini	MV Agusta	2.12.24.4	102.59
2	Peter Williams	Matchless	2.18.03.0	98.4
3	Frank Perris	Suzuki	2.20.45.4	96.51

1971 Junior TT

1	Tony Jefferies	Yamsel	2.05.48.6	89.91
2	Gordon Pantall	Yamaha	2.06.25.0	89.55
3	W A [Bill] Smith	Honda	2.07.04.8	89.09

1972 Senior TT

1	Giacomo Agostini	MV Agusta	2.10.34.4	104.02
2	Alberto Pagani	MV Agusta	2.18.25.8	98.13
3	Mick Grant	Kawasaki	2.20.00.0	97.03

1972 Junior TT

1	Giacomo Agostini	MV Agusta	1.50.56.8	102.03
2	Tony Rutter	Yamaha	1.55.21.4	98.13
3	Mick Grant	Yamaha	1.56.01.0	97.57

1973 Senior TT

1	Jack Findlay	Suzuki	2.13.45.2	101.55
2	Peter Williams	Matchless	2.14.59.4	100.62
3	Charlie Sanby	Suzuki	2.15.27.6	100.27

1973 Junior TT

1	Tony Rutter	Yamaha	1.50.58.8	101.99
2	Ken Huggett	Yamaha	1.52.31.6	100.58
3	John Williams	Yamaha	1.52.49.4	100.32

1974 Senior TT

1	Phil Carpenter	Yamaha	1.56.41.6	96.99
2	Charlie Williams	Yamaha	1.57.31.6	96.31
3	Tony Rutter	Yamaha	1.59.57.4	94.35

1974 Junior TT

1	Tony Rutter	Yamaha	1.48.22.2	104.44
2	Mick Grant	Yamaha	1.50.06.2	102.8
3	Paul Cott	Yamaha	1.51.47.0	101.25

1975 Senior TT

1	Mick Grant	Kawasaki	2.15.27.6	100.27
2	John Williams	Yamaha	2.15.58.8	99.88
3	Chas Mortimer	Yamaha	2.18.22.8	98.15

1975 Junior TT

1	Charlie Williams	Yamaha	1.48.26.4	104.38
2	Chas Mortimer	Yamaha	1.49.51.0	103.04
3	Tom Herron	Yamaha	1.50.35.4	102.35

1976 Senior TT

1	Tom Herron	Yamaha	2.09.10.0	105.15
2	Ian Richards	Yamaha	2.09.13.4	105.11
3	Billy Guthrie	Yamaha	2.09.33.0	104.84

1976 Junior TT

1	Chas Mortimer	Yamaha	1.46.00.2	106.78
2	Tony Rutter	Yamaha	1.46.07.0	106.66
3	Billy Guthrie	Yamaha	1.49.01.8	103.81

INDEX

Also available from The Crowood Press

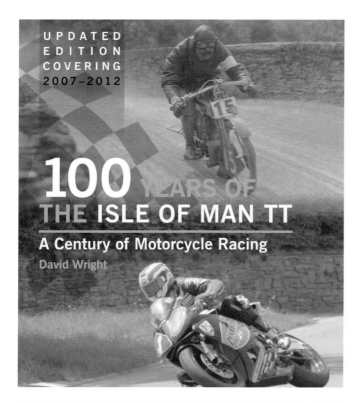

UPDATED EDITION COVERING 2007–2012

100 YEARS OF THE ISLE OF MAN TT

A Century of Motorcycle Racing

David Wright

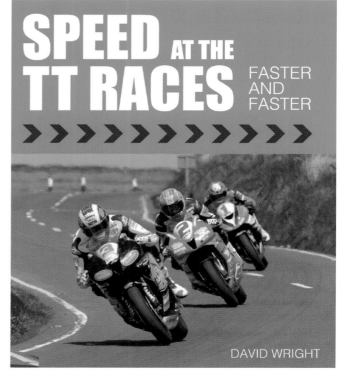

SPEED AT THE TT RACES

FASTER AND FASTER

>>>>>>>>>>

DAVID WRIGHT

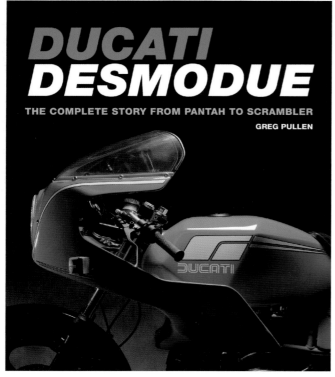

DUCATI DESMODUE

THE COMPLETE STORY FROM PANTAH TO SCRAMBLER

GREG PULLEN

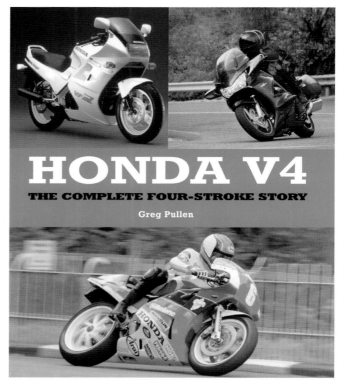

HONDA V4

THE COMPLETE FOUR-STROKE STORY

Greg Pullen